A Play,
A Pie and
A Pint

Volume One

Salamander Street

PLAYS

A Play, A Pie and A Pint Volume One first published in 2020 by Salamander Street Ltd., 272 Bath Street, Glasgow, G2 4JR (info@salamanderstreet.com) www.salamanderstreet.com

Foreword © Morag Fullarton, 2020

Introduction © Joyce McMillan, 2020

Toy Plastic Chicken by Uma Nada-Rajah © 2020*; A Respectable Widow Takes to Vulgarity* by Douglas Maxwell © 2020; *Chic Murray: A Funny Place for A Window* by Stuart Hepburn © 2020; *Ida Tamson by* Denise Mina © 2020*; Jocky Wilson Said* by Jane Livingstone and Jonathan Cairney © 2020; *Do Not Press This Button* by Alan Bissett © 2020

PB ISBN: 9781913630225
E ISBN: 9781913630232

Cover design by Salamander Street

Printed and bound in Great Britain

10 9 8 7 6 5 4 3 2 1

CONTENTS

Foreword

The play's the thing, and since David MacLennan and Colin Beattie joined forces at the Òran Mór in Glasgow in 2004 to create the phenomena that is A Play, A Pie and A Pint, an astonishing 500 new plays have been produced (and counting). Each week for thirty-four weeks of the year a new play is premiered, served up with a pie and a pint, all for around a tenner and performed during your lunch hour. A simple but highly successful formula, the enterprise has fired the imaginations of both emergent and established writers building up an impressive body of new work over the years.

Picking up the baton as joint Artistic Directors in 2016, April Chamberlain and I have had the privilege to work with a fantastic array of writers, overseeing the often fraught, adrenalin fuelled but ultimately rewarding creative process come to fruition on the Òran Mór stage, (after a mere two weeks' rehearsal). The opening day is fondly known by actors as 'shit-a-brick Monday', with good reason!

Many of the plays premiered at PPP, including several featured in this first volume, have gone on to be performed at the Edinburgh Festival, in theatres in London, Paris, New York and beyond, as well as being shown on television. But no amount of electronic wizardry can diminish the magic and creativity of live theatre: each performance is a unique event, a subtle interaction of artistic effort and audience appreciation – or not.

At the time of writing, during the pandemic, all our theatres are dark and there is great concern for the future. But theatre will never die, it is a fundamental activity of mankind; for over two thousand years it has recovered time and again from enforced closures. We will always have stories to tell and wonderful performers to bring them to life, it is an art form that is constantly renewed, and PPP has been at the helm of this tradition for many years now.

I hope you will enjoy reading this first collection of plays as much as we enjoyed bringing them to life. Ultimately, they are there to be performed, it is our firm hope that this first publication inspires new productions.

Morag Fullarton
Artistic Director, July 2020

Introduction

WHEN THE late and much-missed David MacLennan launched A Play, A Pie and A Pint at Òran Mór, Glasgow, in the autumn of 2004, no one – including MacLennan himself – could have guessed at its transformative impact on the production of new work in Scotland, and often far beyond. For MacLennan, it was an act of defiant creativity in the face of an arts funding system that had let him down; in the late 1990s, his radical musical theatre company Wildcat Stage Productions, founded in 1978 as a spin-off from the 7:84 Scotland touring company founded by MacLennan's sister Elizabeth and her husband John McGrath, had lost its regular funding from the Scottish Arts Council, casting MacLennan and his closest colleagues into the theatrical wilderness for several years.

When the Glasgow entrepreneur Colin Beattie moved to open his new bar, restaurant and music venue Òran Mór (the name is Gaelic for Big Song), in a former church on the corner of Byres Road in Glasgow's West End, MacLennan was therefore keen to discuss with him a model for presenting theatre there that would, given in-kind help from the venue, essentially pay for itself, and free MacLennan from the need ever to fill in an arts council application form again; and the formula they devised involved short lunchtime shows, guaranteed to last no more than an hour, and presented along with a drink and a pie, so that even if the audience hated the show, they could at least say they had had a spot of lunch.

MacLennan, in his late fifties, also moved decisively into a new role that turned out to be a true vocation, nurturing new writing across the Scottish theatre scene with a brand-new play every week; and this inspired combination of innovation, risk reduction, and lunchtime conviviality in a part of Glasgow with some disposable income, took off like a theatrical rocket, with the basement nightclub often packed at weekend lunchtimes, and on what became known as 'shit-a-brick Mondays', when small companies of two or three actors – rarely more – would launch a brand-new play with very little rehearsal. MacLennan was skilful at building alliances, notably with theatres in Ireland and Spain, with the new National Theatre of Scotland, and with other theatres around Scotland – including the Traverse in Edinburgh – which began to show an interest in presenting and sometimes co-producing Play, Pie and Pint productions. Within a few years, the Play, Pie and Pint idea was being imitated in theatres from St. Petersburg to Baltimore, and links had been forged as far afield as China;

and the model proved robust enough even to survive David MacLennan's tragic death in 2014, at the age of only sixty-five.

Over the last six years, A Play, A Pie and A Pint has continued to thrive, now with some public funding, first under the direction of young producer Susie Armitage, and later under the joint artistic directorship of April Chamberlain and Morag Fullarton, two veteran Scottish theatre figures in the Wildcat tradition, with – in Fullarton's case – a rare gift for creating theatre that connects with popular culture, and has attracted record audiences to Òran Mór. In 2019, A Play, A Pie and A Pint celebrated its fifteenth birthday and its 500th show, maintaining its production rate of around thirty-five plays a year; and this collection offers a glimpse of the sheer range of the company's work, which still reflects MacLennan's original wish to make space for gifted newcomers, while also allowing more experienced writers, directors and performers to branch out in new directions, and experiment in a low-risk environment.

In this book of texts, which covers shows first produced between 2006 and 2019, you will therefore find plays written by leading Scottish writers who want to try their hand at theatre for the first time – in the case of novelist Denise Mina's *Ida Tamson*, first seen in 2006 – and a leading Scottish playwright trying his hand at a shorter format, as in Douglas Maxwell's hugely entertaining 2013 hit *A Respectable Widow Takes To Vulgarity*. You can see plays about major figures in Scottish popular culture, in Stuart Hepburn's *Chic Murray: A Funny Place For A Window*, by one of Scotland's most experienced actor-screenwriters, and *Jocky Wilson Said*, a Play, Pie and Pint debut play about the world-famous darts champion, by Fife-based brother-and-sister team Jane Livingstone and Jonathan Cairney. And in the two most recent plays, from 2019, you can see both relatively new writer Uma Nada-Rajah, and acclaimed Scottish novelist and playwright Alan Bissett, bringing both wit and passion to some of the most disturbing issues of our time, notably the presence of ingrained institutional racism in Scotland, and the thin veneer of liberal attitudes in the west, easily disrupted by the most minor of threats.

And whatever stage their careers have reached, all of these writers are creating work that matches the Play, Pie and Pint creed laid down by David MacLennan, sixteen years ago; to write briskly, well and entertainingly, in a short format for a small cast, and to create something new, every week.

Over those years, A Play, A Pie and A Pint has transformed the landscape of playwriting opportunities in Scotland, particularly for those who have never written for the stage before. And although not every play presented on that tiny nightclub stage has been a gem, this collection offers an infinitely valuable sense of some of the richness that has been generated, in a decade and a half of A Play, A Pie and A Pint; and of how brilliantly David MacLennan's dream has been fulfilled, in what is now a vital new powerhouse of Scottish theatre-making.

Joyce McMillan
July 2020

A RESPECTABLE WIDOW TAKES TO VULGARITY

Douglas Maxwell

Douglas Maxwell has been one of Scotland's top playwrights since his debut in 2000. His work includes *I Can Go Anywhere* at The Traverse, Edinburgh, *Charlie Sonata* at The Royal Lyceum Edinburgh, *The Whip Hand* for The Traverse/Birmingham Rep, *Yer Granny* (a version of Roberto Cossa's *La Nona*) for the National Theatre of Scotland and *Fever Dream: Southside* for The Citizens, Glasgow.

His many other plays include *Decky Does a Bronco*, *Too Fast*, *Mancub*, *Helmet* and *Promises Promises* (staged in New York as *The Promise*).

His plays have been performed in translation in Germany, Norway, Hong Kong, New York, Chicago, Holland, Canada, Sweden, New Zealand, Wales, Japan, France, Belgium and South Korea, where his debut play *Our Bad Magnet* has run for over ten years.

Douglas lives on the Southside of Glasgow with his wife and two daughters.

A Respectable Widow Takes to Vulgarity was first performed at Edinburgh's The Traverse Theatre during their *Dream Play* series, in August 2012, as a script-in-hand reading.

It had its first full production at Òran Mór, Glasgow, as part of A Play, a Pie and a Pint, co-produced by The Traverse, on Monday 20 February 2013.

Director: Orla O'Loughlin

Cast: Scott Fletcher & Joanna Tope

That production appeared again that summer as a *Breakfast Play* in The Traverse during the Edinburgh Fringe.

It was revived on 1 April 2014, this time with Gavin Jon Wright and Joanna Tope, and again directed by Orla O'Loughlin, in a Traverse production which went to 59E59 in New York.

It was revived again on Monday 18 February 2019 as part of the 500 Play Celebration Season

Director: April Chamberlain

Cast: Anne Kidd & Craig McLean

1.

ANNABELLE LOVE is lost in thought.

She's standing near the door of a TGI Fridays-ish bar/restaurant, holding a glass of white wine but not drinking it. There's a big laugh from inside. A large group of people seem to be very much enjoying her husband's purvey.

She looks towards the racket, but isn't anywhere close to laughing – or grieving.

If she's aloof and formal here, which is no doubt what they are all saying, that is because she is aloof and formal everywhere, not because she has found herself suddenly alone in the world or anything like that. Not really.

JIM DICK, is trying to make a quiet exit from the function. He hurries through the door, shrugging on his coat. He's about twenty years old. He could be ANNABELLE's son, as far as age goes. In no other respect could he be ANNABELLE's son. Mathematically, he could even be her grandson, but no one would believe it.

He breathes a sigh of relief which catches in his throat as he sees ANNABELLE. Worst case scenario, man. Now he's going to have to think of something to say.

As he approaches, ANNABELLE takes his hand… She prides herself on being able to talk to anyone, of any class or background, even in a crisis – like royalty in that respect.

JIM: I'm really sorry about Jo-Jo…eh…Mr Love and that. He was a thingme. A…em…

ANNABELLE: Yes, thank you so much for coming.

JIM: No, he was though.

ANNABELLE: Thank you. It was a beautiful ceremony. Just right… I thought.

JIM: Aye, he was a really, really…

ANNABELLE: It means a great deal to us that so many of the employees have made the effort to be here today. Thank you so very much.

JIM: Oh no worries. Nice to get a day off int it? Eh… No, he was a really, really lovely old cunt.

The handshake freezes. JIM tries to smile it out, but JIM knows. Oh, JIM knows. He aborts everything and bolts off.

2.

In Burger King, across the road, about five minutes later. JIM flops down with his tray, unclips his black tie and shakes his head: what an arsehole, man... He has his burger unwrapped and close to his mouth when he sees ANNABELLE come in through the double-doors. She must've followed him! The burger stays where it is for most of the scene.

ANNABELLE comes over. She still has her wine with her. She sits at his table.

Neither could say for sure what exactly is going on here.

There's a big silence. It doesn't seem to bother her, but it's boiling him alive... Eventually...

JIM:	I'm so sorry. By the way. I really am totally sorry. I didnae mean to kinda, know what I mean? I'm really absolutely... sorry.
ANNABELLE:	You do know there was steak pie at the purvey? Gourmet steak pie. I dread to think how that place defines 'gourmet' but never mind... It's what people want, so I'm told, so there we are. Didn't you like it?
JIM:	It was lovely. A fitting tribute.
ANNABELLE:	But you're still hungry?
JIM:	Naw. Full up.
ANNABELLE:	I've never had a hamburger.
JIM:	I don't even know why I got this. I'll no touch it.
ANNABELLE:	Never really wanted one I suppose.
JIM:	Have this. I'll no touch it.
ANNABELLE:	No, thank you.

JIM:	Aye fair enough. Fucking horrible hing. Sorry. Swearing. Nervous.
ANNABELLE:	How do you know it's horrible if you haven't tasted it?
JIM:	Oh they're always horrible.
ANNABELLE:	But you still eat them?
JIM:	You've just got to get on with it sometimes, sure you have? Is it that I'm sacked?
ANNABELLE:	Sacked? No… Why would you say that?
JIM:	I didn't mean to swear. I'm just rubbish at funerals… I get all kind of fucking…sorry… all kind of fucking…sorry. Shit! (*Controlling breath.*) I went mental at a funeral once. When I was sixteen. I think it's that.
ANNABELLE:	Was it someone terribly close to you?
JIM:	Aye. He was sitting in the same row.
ANNABELLE:	(*Confused.*) What?
JIM:	He passed me a note in the church. Freaked me out to f… Am I sacked, cos it was just a slip of the tongue, know what I mean? I promise I'll never swear again, or something.
ANNABELLE:	What was in the note?
JIM:	I can't tell you. It had swearing in it. Am I sacked?
ANNABELLE:	Okay – what's your name?
JIM:	Jim. Jim Dick. I work in the Depot.
ANNABELLE:	Jim Dick. If you don't tell me what was in that note, the one the chap passed to you in the church when

	you were sixteen and which upset you so much, then yes, you are sacked. Clear?
JIM:	It was such a beautiful ceremony, gourmet steak pie, it seems a shame tae…
ANNABELLE:	Look at me, Jim Dick.

He does.

JIM:	Okay. *(Deep breath.)* There was a guy. He was the spit of Piers Brosnan, this guy. At first I was like that, 'what the hell is Piers Brosnan doing here?' But naw, it wasnae Piers Brosnan.
ANNABELLE:	And he passed you a note?
JIM:	Aye. It was weird cos see up till then, I'd actually forgotten there was anyone apart from me in the church. It was like all the faces and bodies and statues had just, kinda, disappeared. And I was alone, like, in space or something. Me and the coffin and the voice of the minister. Then the note got handed to me. I took it… Read it. Went scripto.
ANNABELLE:	What did it say?
JIM:	…
ANNABELLE:	What did it say?
JIM:	It said… 'I want to love you fuckless'.

Beat.

ANNABELLE:	But…what does that mean?
JIM:	When I could finally look at him he was pure scribbling another note. He got that one passed down too. And it's funny, cos in a way, this other note was worse.

ANNABELLE: Why?

JIM: I think it was the final straw. You cannae tell what the final straw's gonna be can you? It's no really up tae us.

Pause.

ANNABELLE: Jim.

JIM: What?

ANNABELLE: What did the second note say?

JIM: The second note said… 'Not you. Him'. And there was an arrow. Pointing to my Uncle Stevie, who was sitting next to me. That was it… Next thing I remember I'm lying in the road and my mum's shouting at me – saying she's cursed.

Big pause.

ANNABELLE shakes her head. It's a mystery… And talking of mysteries…

ANNABELLE: How can one be 'lovely' and a…you know – what you said about Joseph at the restaurant? How can those two words go together? Was 'lovely' a slip of the tongue too?

Beat.

JIM: Naw. It's no always a hingme… A bad word. I mean, it is. Obviously. I shouldnae've said it. But with Scottish guys it can mean like, a geezer, a lad, a good…kinda…guy.

Big silence.

ANNABELLE: It worries me that such a powerful word may have an undiscovered usage. I fight for the language, Jim. But I have no dominion over those words. It's not that I've never needed vulgarity – it's that I've never *wanted* it… Do you understand? I suppose much in the same way I've never really wanted a hamburger. I think I'd forgotten it was even an option.

JIM: I really wish I hadn't told you that thing about Piers Brosnan now.

ANNABELLE: No. It's fine. And the way you described my husband was fine too. It felt true. You were the only one who managed that today. The only one who even came close. (*The burger.*) May I?

JIM: Wire in.

ANNABELLE takes a bite and savours it for a long time. Longer than necessary really. Eventually…

ANNABELLE: Mm… It's absolutely revolting.

JIM: The barbeque version is worse.

She takes another bite.

3.

The next day.

JIM is humping a stacked pallet of shrink-wrapped goods in the Depot. He's in uniform – polo shirt and cargo trousers – and talking to some offstage guy…

JIM: Fucking, hing is, you cannae just lift some cunt out ay his natural hingme and fucking drop him here and expect him to be as fucking ace as he wis back home, fucking straight away.

Aye, okay, he's a pro, right, getting twenty-five grand a week or something, so he can suck it up, right? Aye. Okay. But also, right, he's a fucking *teenager*. Cunts forget that… He's away fae his family, he's in some big fucking new-build in the middle of fucking nowhere and the only furniture he's got is a fucking Nintendo Switch.

And…and, this my main point…he doesnae speak a fucking word ay English. And this was what I was saying tae that prick Iain, see if you dinnae speak the fucking language, you're fucked. Cos on wan level, you're chapping.

Cunts'll be talking to him like he's a wee dick, cos he cannae understand them, even though, bet you any money, he's ten times smarter than they are, back in his own country. But see if folk think you're thick, *you* start to think you're thick… And if you *think* you're thick, you start to *do* stuff that *is* thick, and before you know it, you're a fucking arsehole… It carries, man. Confidence drops. The head goes down.

It's like aw they cocks in Portsmouth giving it 'aw we can't understand you Scots. You need to speak slower.' I'm like that: naw man, you need tae listen quicker. How come I can understand every fucking thing you say? Geordie, Yorkshire, Cockney, but they cannae even fucking *hear* me… But still, when I put the phone down, I'm the one that feels stupit.

Naw… Give him time man. Let the words come. He gets the words, he'll feel smart again, and that's when he'll start banging in the goals. Fact.

TANNOY   JIM DICK TO THE OFFICE. JIM DICK TO THE OFFICE.

JIM is worried. He drops what he's doing and exits.

4.

In the office. It hasn't been touched since Joseph died. There are reminders everywhere.

ANNABELLE is standing beside the desk when JIM comes in. She has her coat on and is trying to appear breezy and off-the-cuff.

JIM hovers in the doorway, extremely uncomfortable, reverting to the terrified-pupil-in-the-headmaster's-office archetype.

ANNABELLE: Oh hello Jim. Nice to see you again.

JIM: Awright?

ANNABELLE: Just checking in really. Transitional phase this. Mark is moving back of course, but it'll take time for him to find a place, get the girls settled in school and so on. Shouldn't take too long for the business side of things to return to normal. He's lived all his life in logistics so I expect he'll take to it like a duck to water. His heart wasn't in teaching really.

Silence.

ANNABELLE: And how are you?

JIM: Fine.

ANNABELLE: Pardon?

JIM: Fine.

ANNABELLE: Good. And the others? Not too upset?

JIM: What about?

ANNABELLE: About Joseph's passing?

JIM: Aw right. Naw, fine.

ANNABELLE: I was saying to our good friend Cliff – he did the eulogy – that during a lengthy illness one grieves before the death itself, in a sense. I suppose there's

comfort to be taken in that. Life begins again
relatively quickly, so to speak. In that respect.

Another silence.

ANNABELLE: I've told Mark about you.

JIM: What? About me?

ANNABELLE: Yes.

JIM: What about me?

ANNABELLE: Just that you're an intelligent young man and are a
valuable asset to the company.

JIM: About me?

ANNABELLE: Yes.

JIM: Why did you tell him that?

ANNABELLE: Isn't it true?

JIM shrugs.

ANNABELLE: And I had a thought, also, about your story. The
note.

JIM: Aye. Look. Sorry about aw that... I was kinda...

ANNABELLE: No, not at all. No, I had a thought. Could it be,
perhaps, that the note included a comma after the
word 'you'. 'I want to love you' comma 'whatever'...
In that case, grammatically speaking, that would
imply that the word following the comma would be
a proper noun. A name. So rather than... 'fuckless',
it may have been, for instance, Douglas. In your
panic you may have misread. 'I want to love you,
Douglas'.

JIM: Who's Douglas?

ANNABELLE: Piers Bronsan is Douglas

Beat.

JIM: Is that all?

ANNABELLE: Yes.

JIM starts to leave.

ANNABELLE: Oh there was one more thing Jim. I've been wondering too, about cunt.

That stops him.

ANNABELLE: Your little revelation that there is a Scottish usage which is positive rather than negative got my old brain going I'm afraid. I was wondering, would it be correct, for example, if someone was, I don't know, very good at playing the organ, to say: 'Lillian is a cunt on the organ'?

JIM: Eh… no really.

ANNABELLE: Why not?

JIM: It just…sounds a bit…no right.

ANNABELLE: Well how would you say it?

JIM: I dunno.

ANNABELLE: Oh please, speak freely. I find this fascinating. I really do. I fight for the language.

JIM: Well. I think, it's kinda, no right if it's a woman… Know what I mean?

ANNABELLE: Oh I see. Yes of course.

JIM: And it doesnae mean 'good at something'. You'd have to say… 'see that cunt John, he's fucking amazing on the organ'. Or something. I dunno. I kinda need to get back to…

ANNABELLE: Oh of course! I didn't mean to keep you. Thanks awfully Jim. If you ever need anything from me please feel free to ask. I'm at your disposal… Have a very good day.

JIM: Right.

JIM exits, moderately freaked out. ANNABELLE drops her smile when he's gone and after a moment or two, starts to practise…

ANNABELLE: Lillian is fucking wonderful on the organ. Lillian is a fucking wonderful organist… I'll tell you who is a fucking lovely organist – Lillian. Mm. Prefer cunt really.

5.

A doctor's waiting room. JIM is at the desk.

JIM: Will it be Doctor Ito? No, that's fine aye. Just checking. Doctor Ito is wonderful. Fine I mean. Not a problem… Nae tother a baw! Cheers.

JIM takes a seat. He takes off his coat. Picks up a magazine. He's very nervous, his leg is bouncing

After a beat or two…

Nope, this is not gonna happen! He chucks the magazine, grabs his coat and exits…

JIM: *(To the receptionist as he goes.)* Just remembered I'm…better.

6.

ANNABELLE is on the phone.

She's sitting with a note pad in her lap. She's building herself up to something…

ANNABELLE: Yes… Yes, I'm happy to remain Treasurer as long as someone is on hand to help with the parish magazines…

Oh, I know you do Gordon, but especially now I just feel *(Looks at the pad, chickens out.)* enough's enough…

I know…

It is a bit of a *(Looks at the pad, chickens out again.)* faff for just the one person isn't it?…

Much better thank you Gordon. And thank you once again for everything. It was a beautiful ceremony, just right…

Oh, I'd forgotten all about that…

That's a lie. She stands up, primed. This is what she's been waiting for. Can she go through with it though?

The organist is such an important…

Yes, it really lifts the service I feel…

Well, Lillian and Old Mr Swanson are super candidates, and that they're both happy to put themselves forward speaks volumes I think…

Mm, of the two, I'd say the thing that sways it in Lillian's favour, for me, is that she is a…is such a… she's a … when it comes to playing the organ, I would say…I would probably have to say…Lillian is…is…

Old Mr Swanson is fucked, Gordon. So my vote would be for Lillian, but I am open to discussion.

She cringes, braced for a response. It's clear though that Gordon didn't register the word and is carrying on. The wind goes from her sails...

> Yes, that's true. Yes, availability is something we have to consider, especially...

> Yes, that's a very good point Gordon.

ANNABELLE sits, puts the pad to the side and slumps in her chair. Gordon is still talking, but she's not listening any more.

7.

TANNOY JIM DICK TO THE OFFICE. JIM DICK TO THE OFFICE.

A day or two later.

The office is emptier than the last time. Jo Jo's stuff is in cardboard boxes... ANNABELLE sits behind the desk and JIM sits facing her. ANNABELLE seems quite cheery... JIM's a tiny bit easier in her company, but only because he's pissed off.

ANNABELLE: I call them my Jewels. I string them on to my sentences like paste gems on a chain. It's gaudy I admit, but I'm in a gaudy mood these days, so hey ho. Do you know what I've noticed though Jim? No one cares. My friends are clearly not listening to a word I bumming say.

JIM: Look, can I go?

ANNABELLE: I've just got a few wee questions Jim, it won't take a minute. And even Margot, who will walk out of a play at the drop of a shit, did not bat an eyelid, when I asked her if she wanted 'that last fucking French cake'.

JIM: It's just we've got a big shipping set for sign-out at half past.

ANNABELLE:	No it's fine. I told Stefan we had a meeting. So I got to thinking about how we use language – bad language – as a mode of control. Not just to insult, but as a way to pen those who use certain words: 'they are coarse and vulgar, do not regard them!' etc.
	But if people are defeated by a word – squashed and repulsed and shocked by a word – then they lose. Don't they? That's why, I suppose, certain oppressed groups have reclaimed the very insults once thrown at them.
	So I asked myself, what language controls me, oppresses me? The answer? Small talk. Even with my closet friends it's chitter-chatter, chitter-chatter. Of course they don't notice what I'm saying, because for most of my adult life I've been trying my best to say nothing at all. In the name of refinement. So now they're deaf to me. Everyone is. They're just sitting there, nodding to the conversational beat, waiting for the chorus to come along, so they can all join in.
JIM:	Mrs Love, look. Nae offense but…I don't really know you. And really, I didnae know Mr Love either. I know we talked on the funeral day an that, but see me, I've only been here for seven months. I don't know why you…I don't know what you want.
ANNABELLE:	Well… I thought you were interested in all of this?
JIM:	In all what?
ANNABELLE:	Ribaldry. Swearing.
JIM:	Nobody's interesting in swearing, it's not a hing you can be interested in.
ANNABELLE:	Oh it is. For instance, a number of the most commonly used obscenities can be etymologically

traced to five hundred year old farming terms.
That's very interesting, isn't it?

JIM: No.

ANNABELLE: Well did you know the 'safe' word, Berk, is actually cockney rhyming slang? Berkley Hunt. That's interesting. Or…em…here's one: how many times do you think Shakespeare uses the word cunt?

JIM: *(Shrugs.)* None?

ANNABELLE: That's right. But he *punned* on it no less than…

JIM: *(Standing.)* Naw look, you're awright. I need to…I should just go. Okay?

ANNABELLE: Yes, okay. But…please…just…I only have five questions. Please Jim, I can't ask anyone else. Quickly?

JIM sighs and sits back down like a sullen teenager. ANNABELLE happily gets out a piece of paper and reads…

ANNABELLE: One… What's the difference between a dick and a prick?

JIM: Same thing, only a prick's a wee bit more, kinda… Like, em…Boris Johnson's a dick, right? But Donald Trump is a prick. Know what I mean?

ANNABELLE: Yes, good… Two… When to use 'arse' and when to use 'ass'?

JIM: Naw, ass is American. You can use it, but you need to put on a wee voice or else you sound like a fudd.

ANNABELLE: *(Taking notes.)* Fudd. Excellent.

JIM: It's the same with motherfucker. Doesnae sound right in our accent or something. Sounds like you're

acting it. Stick with arse and arsehole... More
traditional.

ANNABELLE: Traditional's good... Three... How to start a
sentence with the word 'fucking'? I've heard you do it
but I just don't seem to have the knack.

JIM: Aye. It's like, gathering your thoughts. 'Fucking...
how come you're picking on me?'

ANNABELLE: 'Fucking...how come you're picking on me?'
Good... Four... What does 'come on tae fuck'
mean?

JIM: It means...kinda...come on...to...come on and...
eh...

ANNABELLE: Don't worry if these are too difficult.

JIM: They're not difficult.

ANNABELLE: Well perhaps it's confusing...

JIM: It's not confusing either...

ANNABELLE: I mean if you don't know, it's fine.

JIM: You think I'm thick don't you?

ANNABELLE: I'm not saying you're...

JIM: I know what 'come on to fuck' means! I've been
thinking it for the last fifteen minutes... What I
don't know is what we're doing here. See when my
dad died, I couldnae get outa bed for a week. But
here's you, happily swearing away to some wee
guy you don't know from fucking Adam, instead of
being at home, with your family, grieving for your
dead husband. What the fuck's wrong with you?

JIM gets up and leaves the office.

After a moment…

ANNABELLE: And Five…How do you think these words? Because I can only say them. But Joseph *thought* them. I know he did. I just want to speak his language… That's all.

She crumples up her notes.

A beat.

The door opens and JIM comes back in, sheepishly.

JIM: 'Come on tae fuck' means, kinda, 'for goodness sake'. There's a phrase, 'come on to grips', meaning, like, 'get a grip'. Over time folk must've changed 'grips' to 'fuck'.

ANNABELLE: *(Small.)* That's what happens with language. It's not erosion – as the didactical would have it – it's growth.

Another couple of beats…

JIM: We can keep talking about this. If you want… It's fine. Just no here, eh? These walls are like cardboard, man. Everyone hears everything.

ANNABELLE: Thank you Jim.

8.

Split scene.

ANNABELLE is on the phone to her son Mark. She's angry.

JIM is back in the doctor's waiting room, flicking through the same magazine as before. He looks calmer this time.

ANNABELLE: No, there has to be another way…

It's far too early Mark. The scope of the business is…the scope of the business…

I do trust you darling but you've been there two minutes how can…?…

Have you consulted Stefan on this? Or Lisa? I'm sure they will be able to come up with alternatives, this is all so new to you…

JIM puts the magazine down. Panic is setting in. He tries to control himself.

ANNABELLE: Well Stefan never mentioned anything like that to me. Your father assured us…

I'm not! I'm just saying…

Yes, I know you are…

Yes, I know you do…

JIM goes over to the reception desk.

JIM: Excuse me where are the toilets?

(Nodding.)

Just there? Right you are.

Beat.

JIM calmly turns in the opposite direction and walks off. His walk accelerates into a run, and once again, he's gone.

ANNABELLE: Oh fuck the economic climate Mark! This is fucking cowardice! It's not what he would've…

I'll tell you what's 'got into me'. Everything. Fucking everything!

Well, perhaps I would listen to reason, Mark, if I heard any reason.

No… I disagree… This is not a time for creative
frugality… This is a time for not being a cunt!

She ends the call.

9.

A few days pass.
They're in Burger King.
ANNABELLE and JIM are both well into their meals.

ANNABELLE: So I've been working on vulgarising my internal
monologue. But it's not going well.

JIM: Aye, it's no easy.

ANNABELLE: How do you get to the point where the words just
spring naturally?

JIM: You just have to let go. Let it all flow out.

ANNABELLE: I'm worried if I let it all flow out, then there might
be a flood… People may drown. For years I've been
saying things like, 'Cliff can go on a bit sometimes
can't he?' and 'Margot is tad old fashioned but her
heart's in the right place'. That kind of thing…
But if I just let it flow, that could so easily become,
'oh fuck off Cliff you boring old prick and take that
racist bitch Margot with you'. But I wouldn't mean
it you see. Not really. I don't want to lose anyone
else.

Beat.

ANNABELLE: Did I tell you about my project?

JIM: Moving in with Mark and that? Aye, sounds good.

ANNABELLE: No. No, that's not…definite. No, my grand
'Jewellery' project. I… am going to invent a new

swear word! One which will sweep the English-speaking world. All I have to do is find something crying out for a descriptive obscenity. But they're impossible to track down. Everything's taken.

JIM: Not everything.

ANNABELLE: I don't mean a synonym for fuck or shit or something. I aim to create a brand-new classification. Corner the market.

JIM: I know something that needs a new swear word.

ANNABELLE: Tell me.

JIM: It's a bit…

ANNABELLE: Oh come on! Bit late in the day to be coy.

JIM: Know how, back in the 90s or something, when there was loads of stuff that was suddenly racist, so folk stopped saying that stuff and got new words instead? Like 'coloured' or 'black affronted'?

ANNABELLE: Is 'black-affronted' racist now? Oh my god!

JIM: Aye… Well, there's one word the whole world has forgotten about. A bit of the body is still racist and totally crying out for a new name.

ANNABELLE: How can a bit of the body be racist?

JIM: Because there's no medical name for that particular bit of the body – only the old racist name. So, like, if that bit was in agony, you couldnae go to the doctor, because she'd think you were a total racist. It's a nightmare.

ANNABELLE: Are you saying there is a part of the body which doesn't have a medical…?

JIM: Nobody knows what to call it! The racist swearword is all we've got.

ANNABELLE: And you've looked this up?

JIM: *(Shakes his head.)* My mum monitors my internet searches. There was a…hing. An incident… Not porn! A feud… In a forum… Got very personal… Police got involved. She's on me like a hawk these days, man. Fuck, I need to get out of that house.

ANNABELLE: Did you look it up in a book?

JIM: Oh aye! There's a book where you can look that shit up in! I wish.

ANNABELLE: Right, c'mon. Let's get this over with.

She motions that now is the time to tell her the word. JIM comes in close, she leans in too. JIM whispers…

JIM: The Jap's Eye. Do you know what that is?

ANNABELLE: Yes. Yes I do.

ANNABELLE goes back to her burger, but has lost her appetite.

JIM: Never been updated! It's a weird oversight.

ANNABELLE: Oh! I've got a great joke. Ready? *(As 'eureka')* Urethra!

She has a good old laugh at that. JIM not so much.

JIM: Eh?

ANNABELLE: *(Same again.)* Urethra!

JIM shrugs. He doesn't get it.

ANNABELLE: It's a play on words. With 'eureka'. You know, Archimedes. In the bath… Oh come on. It's a very funny joke and I don't normally do jokes.

JIM: I don't see…?

ANNABELLE: That's the real name for that part of the body.

JIM: Urethra? Nah… That sounds like a woman thing. Like a tube or something, rather than… an eye.

ANNABELLE: Well at least the doctor would be in the right ballpark – so to speak – without accusing you of being a racist.

JIM: Would they? Definitely? 'My urethra is totally burning.' They'd understand that? And they wouldnae need to look?

ANNABELLE: Well, I think they'd probably still need to look.

JIM: Sake. *(Sigh.)* You fucking cannae win can ye?

Pause. ANNABELLE is about to say something but lets it go.

Change of subject instead…

ANNABELLE: What was your fight all about on the internet?

JIM: Football.

ANNABELLE: Oh.

Another pause.

JIM's has an idea. He can't believe he's about to say this but…

JIM: Hey… I think I know a way for you to let it all go and get the swear words flowing, without anybody drowning.

ANNABELLE: Oooh. I'm intrigued.

JIM:	But, maybe…like…you could…maybe…in return…do me a wee favour?
ANNABELLE:	I dearly hope this doesn't have anything to do with a Jap's Eye?
JIM:	No. Well. Yeah. A little bit.

10.

In the doctor's reception.

ANNABELLE sits with JIM. ANNABELLE is excited. JIM looks doomed.

ANNABELLE:	I am absolutely loving this.
JIM:	I'm no.
ANNABELLE:	It's like Cyrano De Bergerac.
JIM:	I knew you were going to say that.
ANNABELLE:	Do you know what it is?
JIM:	Yes.

Beat.

ANNABELLE:	It's a story about a man with a…
JIM:	I know what Cyrano De Bergerac is Annabelle! Sake.
ANNABELLE:	Sorry. *(Beat.)* Do you want to practise it?
JIM:	No.
ANNABELLE:	And you're sure you don't want me to come in with you?

ANNABELLE gets a very clear answer to that question – in the form of a glare.

ANNABELLE:	It's romantic. Have you learnt the Shakespeare?

JIM:	Aye. I might no do it but.
ANNABELLE:	Do the Keats then. Honestly, she'll be bowled over.
JIM:	She willnae. She'll think I'm just parroting back some bullshit to try to impress her. Which is the truth.
ANNABELLE:	Just make sure you do the speech *after* the examination. Don't say anything before or during.
JIM:	It's just…I think I'm in love with her. I think it's real love. But it's never going to happen is it? It cannae. Like, if it was a film, folk would be going: 'no way! She wouldnae even talk to that wee dick'.
ANNABELLE:	Oh she would! She will. When I first met Joseph he had no qualifications, no belongings and could barely speak a coherent sentence. But he made me laugh and I took a chance. He was nice to me. He liked me and he was kind. That's enough. That's all there is actually! And as time went on, and he grew away for his family and into mine, his speech… *(Beat.)* I've changed my mind. I think you should throw everything I wrote for you in the bin. Talk to her in your own words.
JIM:	No! My own words are shit. Plus, I've learnt it now. *(Different voice.)* 'I realise that this may be highly inappropriate, but I'm not sure I could live with the enormity of never having shared with you the thoughts of a poet who felt as I do when he wrote: 'Doth…?'
VOICE	JIM DICK! JIM DICK!
JIM:	Shit.

JIM stands, like a man off to the gallows.

He takes a deep breath and heads towards the doctor's office.

ANNABELLE: Wait! Jim. Don't. I'll get you in to see my doctor about…your…you know. He's a family friend. Expensive, but…my treat. Come back to her when there's nothing really wrong… Then make her laugh. And be kind.

JIM looks betrayed.

Then, after a beat…

JIM: Thank fuck, let's go!

JIM heads for the exit, followed by ANNABELLE.

As they go…

ANNABELLE: What about spouter?

JIM: Who's Spouter?

ANNABELLE: For Jap's Eye?

JIM: No.

ANNABELLE: Slit-tube?

JIM: Nah.

ANNABELLE: Piss-Gub?

JIM: No way.

ANNABELLE: Pee-Maw?

JIM: Pee-Maw?

11.

A huge crowd roars.

JIM and ANNABELLE are at a football match.

JIM:	On you go.
ANNABELLE:	Should I just start?
JIM:	Aye.
ANNABELLE:	And nobody will mind?
JIM:	Look around.
ANNABELLE:	But what kind of thing?
JIM:	*(Shouting at the top of his voice.)* Oh come on tae fuck man that's pish! Fuck sake!
ANNABELLE:	*(Laughs.)* Oh god. I won't know what to say.
JIM:	Wait till everyone jumps up and then just say whatever comes into your head.

The game goes on. There are one or two false starts, but it doesn't take long before there's an incident. The crowd leaps to its feet – as does ANNABELLE.

ANNABELLE:	*(Screaming.)* Fuck off you fucking devils! You're an ugly arse! Go to hell! I hate you!

She sits down, exhilarated… JIM laughs.

JIM:	That was ace!
ANNABELLE:	That *was* ace. I'm doing it again. *(Screaming.)* Pricks! Piss clown! Shut up! *(To JIM.)* And they don't mind?
JIM:	They're professionals.
ANNABELLE:	Even if they hear you?
JIM:	They cannae hear you.

ANNABELLE: I'm going to shout at one when he gets really close. God this is good. *(Standing and screaming at one player, presumable at close range.)* Fucking ballbag! What the Christ are you wanking at? Get away from me you fatso! You're nothing but a dirty, stinking Catholic pig!

This last remark has an immediate effect on JIM, but not ANNABELLE, until…

ANNABELLE: *(To JIM.)* Oh god! He's looking up. I think he heard me. *(She gives the player a little wave and sits.)* I think he heard me. Why's everyone looking up?

JIM is serious, staring straight ahead…

JIM: Why did you say that?

ANNABELLE: What?

JIM: The thing about him being a Catholic.

ANNABELLE: I thought that's what you say at football matches.

JIM: That's what you *don't* say!

ANNABELLE: That man in the luminous coat is pointing at us.

JIM: Fuck. Shit. Shit!

ANNABELLE: What's going to happen?

A beat of panic. JIM gets up.

JIM: Listen, I'm away.

ANNABELLE: What?

JIM: You'll be all right getting home?

ANNABELLE: No! I don't know where we are.

JIM:	Just follow folk. You'll be fine.
ANNABELLE:	You're not leaving me here? Please don't leave me here.
JIM:	*(Losing his temper.)* I never told you tae say that! What did you have to say that for? What have you done? Shit, here he comes. I…I'll see you.

JIM leaves.

ANNABELLE:	Jim! Don't leave me… Jim!

ANNABELLE is terrified. There's another huge roar from the crowd. She stays seated.

12.

A few days later.

In the office. It is completely empty now, except for a desk and a chair. ANNABELLE signs a document, puts it an envelope and leaves it on the desk. She goes to leave. She looks serious.

JIM appears at the door, slightly out of breath.

JIM:	Annabelle.
ANNABELLE:	Jim.
JIM:	You all right?
ANNABELLE:	Well. I've just signed an extremely unpleasant document and will probably never set foot in this building ever again. So no. Not really.
JIM:	I'm so sorry. I shouldnae have left you. I feel hellish.
ANNABELLE:	Don't. It was my fault.
JIM:	Aye, but I took you there. And to run away like that.
ANNABELLE:	Please don't blame yourself. I'm an adult.

JIM:	See, I've had season tickets since I was seven… Me and my dad…
ANNABELLE:	I completely understand…
JIM:	I've kept his ticket on, and it's kind of our place even though I know it's just an empty seat, but I cannae risk…
ANNABELLE:	Of course. I was at fault. I behaved grotesquely.
JIM:	What happened? What did they say? Did you get into trouble?
ANNABELLE:	Well, they took me to an office. At first I thought, 'here is a chance for me to put all my recent discoveries into practice. I'll swear my way out! Appeal to them on their own level'. But of course I didn't. The world doesn't work like that. As we all know.
	Instead I turned on the full-beams of my most brittle cadence and slammed them with my language. I was the respected widow! I was outraged! I was falsely accused! They apologised and let me go.
	Needless to say I felt like a thief. And a fool… And I cried a bit and thought, 'Enough. Let's call a halt to all this nonsense and move on, shall we?'
	There's going to be redundancies Jim, I'm afraid.
JIM:	Aye. Some of the boys were saying.
ANNABELLE:	I've spoken to Mark. He promised me that your job is safe. If you want it.
JIM:	What? Why?
ANNABELLE:	Why?

JIM:	I was bad to you though.
ANNABELLE:	No, you weren't.
JIM:	I don't deserve it.
ANNABELLE:	Ach, I don't know if 'deserve' has much to do with anything really. I do know that I've very much enjoyed your company and you've helped me a great deal these last few weeks. More than anyone else. So I want to say thank you. And sorry.
	Let me do this for you. I can do little else.
	But I think we've come to the end of our little friendship. Don't you?
JIM:	No more burgers?
ANNABELLE:	I don't think so. It's been nice knowing you Jim Dick.
JIM:	Aye. Nice knowing you.

They shake hands.

ANNABELLE:	Goodbye.
JIM:	Goodbye.

13.

Burger King.

Weeks, maybe months later.

JIM and ANNABELLE's farewell hasn't taken. Somewhere along the line they must have reconnected, because here they are, surrounded by the debris of burgers and fries and milkshakes, in the middle of a comfortable conversation.

ANNABELLE has a different hairstyle and JIM is wearing a shirt and tie.

JIM:	I just don't think it's funny.
ANNABELLE:	I agree.
JIM:	Folk cannae help their name can they?
ANNABELLE:	No… You know Charles Dickens? The writer?
JIM:	Oh Charles Dickens *the writer*? Not Charles Dickens the IT Consultant? Aye, Annabelle, I know Charles Dickens the writer.
ANNABELLE:	Well I don't know what people know. Anyway, Charles Dickens had a rude name. Very rude actually. The word 'dickens' was the Victorian equivalent of 'cock'. I always thought the reason all his characters had silly names was that *he* had a silly name.
JIM:	I thought it was because his books were published, like, over two years or something, and folk needed a way to remember who everyone was.
ANNABELLE:	Or that, yes. Dick's not too bad. I've heard worse. Joseph had a contact in America with a name that everyone thought was absolutely hilarious. I couldn't see the joke myself.
JIM:	I wouldnae think it's hilarious… Names just arenae funny. Try going to a football summer camp when you're ten, no knowing anyone, and then when they

read out aw the names and get to 'Dick' you've got to put your hand up. See if you think names are funny after that. Hey, talking about funny, did you get that thing I texted you last night?

ANNABELLE: *(Dry.)* Yes thank you, very good. *(Beat.)* God, 'texted' has got to be the ugliest word in the language hasn't it? I just can't get used to 'text' as a verb. Or 'awesome', meaning good. Those words are gone from me.

The older you get the more words just go. I don't mean you forget them, although that too is a problem. I mean the meanings of words change… It's like a little earthquake. The ground shifts out from under you, and nothing will ever be entirely solid again.

You see, when a word changes meaning, you cannot change with it. You simply can't use the word in the new sense. 'That was awesome' or 'I'll text you' and so on… No. I can't do it. So I just let them go. Never say them… They disappear. I've lost so many now.

And the thing is, one feels…cheated. Like when someone dies, you feel cheated. Do you know what I mean? Even though that person may have been dying for years and that moment is all you've thought of, day and night…when it finally comes, you're not just shocked, you're cheated.

I wasn't ready Jim. I just wasn't ready.

JIM: You miss him eh?

ANNABELLE: I don't just miss him. I fucking miss him. I fucking miss my husband.

JIM: Aye. I fucking miss my dad.

JIM takes ANNABELLE's hand. After a beat or two she gathers herself again.
JIM confidently steers them back…

JIM: So what was this funny name then? Worse than Dick?

ANNABELLE: I don't think it's funny at all.

JIM: I'll no find it funny anyway. I think people that laugh at names are a bit… know what I mean?

ANNABELLE: Yes. And he was a lovely old chap too.

JIM: What was his name?

ANNABELLE: Willie Sprinkles.

JIM instantly bursts out laughing.

JIM: Willie Sprinkles?! Ha ha ha!!!

ANNABELLE: It's a perfectly normal name that just happens to…

JIM: No way! Ha ha ha ha! Willie Sprinkles?!!! Ha ha ha ha! No way! Ha ha ha ha! No way!

JIM can't stop laughing.

ANNABELLE is laughing a little too, but at JIM…

ANNABELLE: You said you weren't going to laugh!

JIM: I know! But…Willie Sprinkles! You're laughing too!

ANNABELLE: *(Realising, happily…)* Yeah. I am. I am.

The End.

TOY PLASTIC CHICKEN

Uma Nada-Rajah

Based on a true story

Uma Nada-Rajah is a playwright and staff nurse based in Kirknewton, Scotland. She is one of the BBC's Scottish Voices 2020 and was most recently the Starter Female Political Comedy writer-in-residence at the National Theatre of Scotland.

Uma is a graduate of École Philippe Gaulier and is a previous participant of the Traverse Theatre's Young Writers' Program. She is a winner of the New Playwrights Award from Playwrights' Studio Scotland.

Toy Plastic Chicken was first performed at Òran Mór as part of A Play, A Pie and A Pint on Mon, 6 May, 2019.

Cast: Neshla Caplan, David James Kirkwood and Anna Russell-Martin

Directed by Paul Brotherston

Producer Sarah MacFarlane

Assistant Producer Isabella Bassett

Assistant Director Joanna Bowman

Sound Design Andy Cowan

Lighting Design Ross Kirkland

& Chris Reilly

Designers Jonathan Scott & Gemma Patchett

Special Animatronic Effects Matthew Green

An earlier version of the script, entitled *Magical Plastic Chicken* was first performed on 31 May at the Old State Cinema, Leith as part of the Hidden Door Festival 2018.

The cast was as follows:

RACHEL Habiba Saleh

EMMA Kim Chapman

ROSS Robbie Aitken

THE CHICKEN Gus Maitland

Directed by Uma Nada-Rajah & Tomás Palmer

Production Design Matt Green

Original Composition Luke Sutherland

Stage Management Dot Wheelan

Lighting Design Kate Bonney

Featuring Airline Hostesses: Tilly Gifford, Hannah Downie, Andy Peppitte & Robbie Birrell

SYNOPSIS

At Edinburgh Airport, a toy plastic chicken is suspected to
be a bomb. A woman is screened for domestic radicalisation,
while her interrogators decide to perform violent and radical
act of their own. Based on a true story, *Toy Plastic Chicken* is a
blackly comedic exploration of degradation and revolt.

CHARACTERS

EMMA, a white female in her late twenties.
RACHEL, a female of colour in her late twenties
ROSS, a white male in his late twenties
CHICKEN (voice only)

SETTING

With the exception of the prologue, the action takes place in
real time in Edinburgh Airport.

NOTES

– an interruption
/ overlapping dialogue

PRODUCTION NOTES

A suitable toy plastic chicken is available
from the on-line vendor alibaba.com

PROLOGUE

Lights up on a battery-operated toy plastic chicken. RACHEL walks on stage and goes to pick it up. The chicken suddenly comes to life. It waddles forward mechanically, wings lighting up in a multitude of colours. It plays an outdated pop song with poor quality sound. RACHEL laughs.
Blackout.

ONE

Edinburgh Airport.

A new 'Enhanced Preliminary Security Counter'. There are two stainless steel tables, a baggage scanner, an arch for scanning people and a small counter.

EMMA and ROSS are performing routine checks before opening their security counter. EMMA can't be bothered. ROSS can.

RACHEL enters carrying a handbag with the chicken sticking out of the top.
She stops at a baggage size-checker and attempts to shove her bag in. It doesn't fit.
She needs to re-arrange her bags. She is almost within earshot of EMMA and ROSS.
Throughout the dialogue below, RACHEL is attempting to get her bag to fit in the checker.

EMMA: Fuck my life.

ROSS: Cheer up, Emma. We've got a job to do.
  We are the guardians. We are the front lines. We're like modern-day foot soldiers. Here to –

EMMA: – Here to protect people from their own toothpaste.

OVERHEAD ANNOUNCEMENT: Welcome to Edinburgh Airports' Enhanced Preliminary Screening Service. Remember, if you see anything that doesn't look right, please report it to a member of our team.

EMMA: *(Speaking to Announcement.)* Please dinnae. Because I honestly cannae be arsed.

ROSS: You smell different today.

EMMA: Oh? … It's a new perfume.

ROSS: What's it called?

EMMA: I don't know.

ROSS: How do you no ken what it's called?

EMMA: …? it's called like 'pink' something or other…

ROSS: How do you walk into a shop. Pick up a bottle of perfume. Have a wee sniff. Decide 'Aye I quite fancy that'. Go to pay for it. And not see what it's called.

EMMA: Will you give over?

ROSS: See I buy a perfume because of what it's called. Cold Water. Nah. Sauvage. No chance. Boss. That'll do.

EMMA: It's not my perfume.

EMMA takes out a compact and touches up her under-eye make-up.

OVERHEAD ANNOUNCEMENT: See it? Say it. Sorted.

ROSS: Where the hell's Mackay?

EMMA: … Mackay's not coming in today.

ROSS: What?

EMMA: He called in sick.

ROSS: Sickie on a Sunday morning. Classic Mackay. You'd think he'd show some enthusiasm for the new promotion.

EMMA: Got a cold or something.

ROSS: The type of cold where he's been out on the lash, woke up battered tae fuck and popped too many prescription painkillers to string a sentence together. *(Beat.)* Wait. How do you know he's called in sick?

EMMA: … He, uh, messaged me.

ROSS: He messaged you?

EMMA: Yeah

ROSS: What a cock. What an absolute cock. The other day, right? I went to get a can of juice. I took my phone out for half a second and lo and behold Mackay appears like some arsehole genie in a bottle: "Ross, I'm sure you're familiar with our mobile phone policy?" Aye I am ye fuckin dickhead that's why I was clearly attempting to hide behind the vending machine. "Ross, do I need to remind you of the three 'P's of professionalism?" He's fuckin obsessed with Professionalism, the pathetic patronizing penis. But ye ken what he's like. Ye never know when he's put too many steroids in his smoothie and he's about tae go through the roof. So I'm all: "Aye, Sorry Mackay, phone rule slipped my mind". "… If you wouldnae mind-could ye remind me what the 3P's of professionalism are again?" Thought I'd flatter his ego. Mackay looks at me. "Right, Ross. The 3 P's of professionalism." *(Silence.)* And then there's this silence. He's gone and forgotten them. And in the heat of the moment I cannae mind them either else I couldae pretended to 'chip in'. I'm thinkin he's gonna batter me. First I've gone and broke the mobile phone rule then I've gone and humiliated him. He's stood there. Raging. Breathing's getting all shallower, nostrils all flaring like a wild animal: I had to bolt for my life. But then when *he* doesnae feel like coming in on a Sunday. He bloomin' texts you?? *(Beat.)* Direct contravention of the mobile phone policy.
Just… unprofessional.

EMMA: You were the best candidate for that promotion, Ross. You're the one that reads all the policies. Does all that online learning crap.

ROSS: Management made their decision. I'm not bothered about Mackay. I'm honestly not bothered.

EMMA: *(Under her breath.)* Well, if there's one thing you can say about Mackay: he gets what he wants.

ROSS: It's not just about what people want.

EMMA: What else is it about?

ROSS: Time. Timing. It's about waiting for the perfect moment.

EMMA: There's no such thing as the perfect moment, Ross. There's just, moments. And they just slip past you, all the time. Ken. Until you just shrivel up and die. *(EMMA checks her watch.)* Let's go. That's time.

OVERHEAD ANNOUNCEMENT: Preliminary Screening Counter 'C' is now open for express screening. Could all passengers please form an orderly queue behind the yellow line.

RACHEL looks up. Proceeds to the counter. She approaches the yellow line. Having re-distributed her luggage to meet requirements, the plastic chicken is now tucked under her arm wrapped in a scarf.

ROSS: You may approach the counter. *(RACHEL approaches the counter.)* Documents, please.

RACHEL hands ROSS a British passport. He examines the exterior. He flips through the passport and takes a small magnifying glass out of his pocket to take a closer look. He arrives at the page with her photograph. He examines the photograph. He examines her face.)

Can you tilt your head slightly to the right, please?

ROSS: Is that a birth mark?

RACHEL: Yes.

ROSS: And where are you intending to travel to today?

RACHEL: To Istanbul.

ROSS: And what is the purpose of your travel?

RACHEL: Leisure.

ROSS: What kind of leisure?

RACHEL: Um, a holiday.

ROSS: A holiday. With family or friends…?

RACHEL: Friends…

ROSS: Friend or friend-s?

RACHEL: Friend-s.

ROSS: And what is the intended duration of your holiday with friend-s?

RACHEL: A week and half.

ROSS: Ten days?

RACHEL: Yeah, I guess.

ROSS: You guess?

RACHEL: Ten days.

ROSS: If you'll place your wallet, mobile phone, the contents of your
pockets and any electronic devices into the tray and step through the
scanner.

*RACHEL empties the contents of her pockets into the tray. Her headphones remain
around her neck. The toy plastic chicken remains tucked under her arm.*

EMMA: Your shoes.

RACHEL: They're just flip flops.

EMMA: There was a shoe bomber, mam.

*RACHEL takes off her flip flops. ROSS sends the tray through the scanner.
EMMA scrutinizes the screen.*

EMMA: Clear.

ROSS: You may step through the detector.

*RACHEL steps through the arch of the detector. The chicken sets off the alarm. It
is loud and disconcerting.*

RACHEL: *(Suddenly, lights flash from underneath the scarf. The chicken is laying an egg.)* Oh. Sorry. It's just a…

ROSS: *(Into his walkie talkie.)* Come in!? This is Bravo. CODE 17. This is a CODE 17.

The sounds of a lockdown. Fire exits snap shut.

RACHEL: No, no! It's a chicken. It's just a toy chicken!

(RACHEL fumbles to unwrap the chicken.)

ROSS: Don't lie to me. Don't you bloody lie to me!

RACHEL: I'm not lying!

ROSS: Drop it! Drop it now!

EMMA: No! Wait! Don't drop it!

RACHEL drops the chicken. EMMA and ROSS cover their heads. Nothing happens. Silence. EMMA and ROSS re-emerge. Suddenly, there is movement from beneath the scarf. EMMA screams and they cover their heads once again. The chicken is laying another egg.

ROSS: What's under that sheet??

RACHEL: It's just –

ROSS: – WHAT THE FUCK IS IT AND WHAT THE FUCK IS IT DOING?

RACHEL: It's a toy plastic chicken and it is laying an egg.

RACHEL slowly bends down and unwraps the chicken from the scarf.

I got it from the market this morning. I swear to God.

WALKIE TALKIE: *(Beep!)* Come in Bravo. Zone 24 lockdown initiated. What is your status? I repeat, what is your status.

EMMA picks up the walkie talkie. She looks at ROSS. She looks at RACHEL.

ROSS: Unconfirmed.

EMMA: *(Speaking into the walkie talkie.)* Unconfirmed.

ROSS: It was laying an egg?

RACHEL: It was laying an egg.

ROSS: What… spontaneously?

RACHEL: The guy said it had some sort of defect.

ROSS: Open it.

RACHEL: What?

ROSS: Open the chicken.

RACHEL: But…

ROSS: I said open the flipping chicken!!!

EMMA: Ross…

RACHEL: *(RACHEL crouches down in front of the chicken.)* I… I'd need a screwdriver.

EMMA: Just put it through the scanner, Ross.

> *ROSS looks at EMMA. He looks at RACHEL.*
> *He carefully picks up the chicken and puts it through the scanner.*
> *Silence. EMMA watches the screen intently. She pauses the conveyor belt. Stares.*

WALKIE TALKIE: *(Beep!)* Team Bravo come in.

EMMA: Clear. It's a false alarm.

WALKIE TALKIE: *(Beep!)* Team Bravo: What is your status?

EMMA: This is Bravo. That was a false alarm. Stand down. I repeat stand down.

WALKIE TALKIE: *(Beep!)* Team Bravo that was a false alarm under CODE 17. We're going to need a full report filed by the end of your shift today.

EMMA: *(Groans.)* There's going to be an inquiry.

ROSS: Fuck's sake! *(ROSS grabs the walkie talkie out of EMMA's hands.)*

ROSS: Given, ah, extenuating circumstances, Team Bravo recommends a full Code 3 follow-up under Schedule 7.

WALKIE TALKIE: Copy that.

EMMA: Ross-! You can't do that. She's –

RACHEL: Am I in some sort of trouble?

TWO

The remainder of the play is set in two adjoining rooms: one room is used for interrogation, the other is a sound-proof 'assessment room', for the sole use of security staff. The rooms are separated by a see-through wall which is dominated by a one-sided mirror. The audience should be able to see the action in both rooms simultaneously.

EMMA and ROSS enter the interrogation room followed by RACHEL. EMMA, carrying RACHEL's luggage, heads straight into the assessment room.

ROSS: Make yourself comfortable. *(Gestures for RACHEL to sit down.)* Have a seat.

RACHEL: I'm alright standing.

A tense silence, ROSS and RACHEL look at each other.

ROSS: Sit down.

ROSS and RACHEL hold each others' gaze. RACHEL contemplates.

She sits on the very edge of the chair.

ROSS, hesitates, decides to leave it and exits into the assessment room.

As soon as ROSS has exited, RACHEL springs back up, takes stock of her surroundings.

Next door in the assessment room, EMMA slams RACHEL's luggage down on the table and begins to sort through it.

ROSS takes the chicken out of the bag, examines it briefly and sets it down.

EMMA is extremely annoyed with ROSS.

ROSS: I get the feeling you might be pissed off with me. *(Beat.)* C'mon, Emma, talk to me.

EMMA: I cannae. I'm fantasizing about killing you.

ROSS: 'Least I've finally got you fantasizing about me. *(EMMA gives him a look of death.)* Look. I'm doing you a favour.

EMMA: A favour, Ross? In what possible universe is this a favour? A favour would have been to have taken one look at me and seen that I what I really needed today was a nice, easy shift. *(EMMA examines a hard copy of* Prevent.*)* We're not even properly qualified to be doing this. We're meant to be supervised.

ROSS: Mackay's not in. We're following orders. Emma, this is an opportunity.

EMMA: *(Sarcasm.)* An opportunity.

ROSS: Aye. To get in there with head office.

EMMA: Look, you're never gonna get promoted, Ross! You're not enough of a dick. *(Beat.)* What are we even meant to be doing here?

ROSS: Look. Fine. We called a False Alarm under a Code 17. But – We can use this to carry out a random screening for domestic radicalisation under *Prevent*.

EMMA: What?

ROSS: Prevent. We're meant to be engaging with it across the sector. Dinnae worry. I've done the e-learning module. *(EMMA rolls her eyes.)* Look, all we have to do is suss out which of the criteria she meets, file a report to head office and we're done. Easy as. Next time promotions come round, our report will catch their eye –

EMMA: – Catch their eye? Ross we've just called a Code 17 over a Toy. Plastic. Chicken. And now you've just called for a follow-up under Schedule 7 of the Terrorism Act. On a holiday maker. Whose stuff is completely normal! *(EMMA holds up a bikini.)* The only eye we're going to catch is the sob-story editor of the *Guardian*.

ROSS: What actually happened doesn't matter, Emma. It's the report that matters.

EMMA: There's nothing to put in the report.

ROSS: Sure there is. You're not looking hard enough.

ROSS discovers a postcard image of wildcats in amongst RACHEL's possessions. He holds it up.

ROSS: Aha! See?

EMMA: It's a picture of cats.

ROSS: I've read about this on-line. There's evidence of a correlation between affinity for wildcats and deviant behaviour. Black panthers. Tamil tigers. Et cetera. Any wildcat paraphernalia can and should be treated as suspect.

EMMA: What about domestic cat paraphernalia?

ROSS: That depends on the cat. See this? This is going in the report.

EMMA: What a load of shite.

ROSS: You'll be thanking me when you have an extra two grand in your pocket at the end of the year. *(ROSS looks into the opposite room.)* Besides. She ain't bad looking.

EMMA: You disgust me.

ROSS: I'm just joking.

(Beat.)

You're right. I'm a selfish bastard. Look. You dinnae need this. I do.
    … I mean you could be anything. You know the first time I saw you I honestly thought: What is she doing here? You could be the weather girl? Or in the Olympics. Or an optician or anything. Anything you wanted. This is just a shite job for you. It's cunts like me that need a promotion.

EMMA: Thanks, Ross. Right. Let's have a look.
(Clears her throat.)
"List of possible Indicators of Domestic Radicalization:
Low self-esteem. Sense of Isolation. Migration.
Searching for answers to questions about identity, faith and belonging. An underlying psychological tendency towards deviance or the glorification of violence.
Criticism of British foreign policy. Perceived injustice. Unmet aspirations". *(Beat.)* Unmet aspirations? That's a bit harsh isn't it?
"Family tensions. Criminality. Domestic Violence.
'Having a sense of grievance that is triggered by personal experience of racism, discrimination or aspects of government policy". *(EMMA flips the page. Eyes widen.)* Jesus. It goes on for another half an hour and then it says: "This list is not exhaustive."

ROSS: Let's just do up to there. Here, I'll start. Let's use that as a list of tick-boxes. To keep us on track.

EMMA: Fine. I'll finish trawling through her stuff.

ROSS: *(ROSS doubles back to pick up the toy chicken.)* You know who likes chicken?

EMMA: Who?

ROSS: Mackay. Mackay likes chicken. Puts chicken in his power smoothie.

EMMA: That's disgusting.

ROSS: Ken. See you on the other side.

ROSS exits into the interrogation room.

THREE

EMMA continues to search RACHEL'S luggage in the Assessment Room.
ROSS enters into the interrogation room with RACHEL. He sets the chicken down on the table.

RACHEL: Can we please hurry this up? I'm going to miss my flight.

ROSS: Unfortunately, we have more pressing concerns at the moment. You are being detained under Schedule 7 of the Terrorism Act.

RACHEL: … What? *(Pause.)* I'm not a terrorist.

ROSS: No one said you were.

RACHEL: You just said…

ROSS: That's just what the act is called. It could be called anything.

RACHEL: It's a toy chicken.

ROSS: Under Schedule 7 there is no need for there to be any reasonable cause for an inquiry to proceed to this stage.
In fact, this is completely random.

RACHEL: But this isn't random.

ROSS: I've just said it was random.

RACHEL: We're here because you got freaked out by my toy chicken.

ROSS: You were told to put all electronic devices into a plastic tray.

RACHEL: … Look, I'm sorry. I sincerely apologize for any trouble my toy chicken may have caused. This trip means a lot to me. If I don't catch my flight, I may miss the boat, and –

RACHEL stands as if preparing to leave.

ROSS: – Failure to co-operate with Schedule 7 proceedings is a criminal offense and may result in a fine or up to three months in prison. Or both. Do you understand?

RACHEL: *(Slumps back down.)* ... I've been looking forward to this for ages.

ROSS: Says here you're a care worker.

RACHEL: Yes.

ROSS: Are you aware that ten years ago there was an attempted terrorist attack on Glasgow airport?

WOMAN: Yeah.

ROSS: Then you must also be aware that eight of the ten perpetrators of the attack were health care providers.

WOMAN: Yes?

ROSS: So you can see why we may exert a degree of caution when dealing with people from your line of work. *(Pause.)* I take it you like chickens.

RACHEL: Yes. Well, no.

ROSS: You don't like chickens?

RACHEL: No. I don't know.

ROSS: I'm not trying to trip you up.
For the sake of this investigation it would be helpful to know that, say, you bought this toy chicken because you like chickens. Now. Do you or do you not like chickens? *(RACHEL shakes her head, 'no'. ROSS sighs.)* You don't like chickens. Now, if you don't like chickens. Why do you have in your possession toy plastic chicken?

RACHEL: I bought it as a gift.

ROSS: You buy things for people that you yourself don't like.

RACHEL: It's not that I don't like chickens.

ROSS: You just told me that you don't like chickens.
C'mon. Level with me here. I'm not going to bite. I promise.

RACHEL: I had a bad experience.

ROSS: A bad experience.

RACHEL: When I was eight, I microwaved a live chicken.

ROSS: You what?!

RACHEL: It's not… well. When I was little, we stayed out in the countryside. My ma used to keep chickens out in the back garden. After she died, my dad took to drinking. He had an air rifle, right, and he and his pal would sometimes go hunting, shooting rabbits, having a few beers and that. One day, they were halfway out the door when my big brother piped up and asked if he could go along with them. My dad's pal was just like aye sure why no. So I asked if I could go. But my dad says no. I begged. Still no. He wasn't having it. I was gutted. And absolutely raging. So after they left, I decided I was gonna go hunting myself. I was gonna be part of the gang. I got myself a big black bin bag and climbed into the chicken pen. Threw the bin bag over one of the chickens and caught it. It went mental all thrashing about and I didn't know what to do, so I tied the bag shut and ran inside. Guess I thought I would cook it. Like my ma would've done. I shoved the chicken in the microwave. Bag and all.
Must have thought, that's what you do. Then I pressed the buttons. All at once. I will never forget the sounds that came out of that microwave. I went and hid in the closet. When my dad came home, he went and opened the microwave and was sick all over the kitchen counter.

ROSS: Jesus.

RACHEL: And to this day, I do not like, eat, or associate with chickens. But I saw this chicken in the market today. All covered in shiny plastic and flashing lights. Guess I forgot it was even a chicken. I bought it against my better judgement.

ROSS: Well, you know what they say: A chicken is a chicken is a chicken.

RACHEL: I've not heard anyone say that before.

ROSS: I've got a few more questions for you. Now. To the best of your knowledge. Would you say you suffer from low self-esteem?

RACHEL: Um. No. Not really.

ROSS: *(ROSS hesitates. Puts a cross in his tick box.)* Do you ever feel, um… lonely?

RACHEL: What is this even about?

ROSS: How do you feel about British foreign policy?

RACHEL: I don't know. It's fine.

ROSS: You're going to need to give me more than that. Let's take Syria, for example. What are your views on the situation in Syria?

RACHEL: I don't know.

ROSS: You don't know. What do you think, when you think about Syria?

RACHEL: … I think it's sad.

ROSS: Sad. Good. Why do you think it's sad?

RACHEL: Because children are dying.

ROSS: Have you ever had the impulse to take action on the issue of Syria?

RACHEL: I believe the correct answer is no. I've never had the impulse to take action on the issue of dying children in Syria.

ROSS: I didn't ask you for the correct answer. I asked you for your answer.

RACHEL: … No.

ROSS: Good. Okay. *(ROSS ticks a box.)* How do you feel about the political situation here in Scotland?

RACHEL: I don't know. It's fine?

ROSS: − Do you perceive that there is any injustice? … Beyond the normal levels.

RACHEL: *(Sarcastic.)* Well not beyond the 'normal levels'.

ROSS: Give me an example.

RACHEL: Like when I see a homeless person on the street?

ROSS: Like when you see a homeless person on the street.

RACHEL: When I see a homeless person on the street, there's a moment, where I might feel sad.

ROSS: Right. And then?

RACHEL: Then I tell myself that I am too busy, that I shouldn't give them time or money because they'll just spend it on drugs. I do exactly what I'm conditioned to do.

ROSS: You could give money to charity.

RACHEL: *(Blandly.)* Sometimes I give money to charity.

ROSS: That's nice. Now. Say if we were to ask you where you were from. What would you say?

RACHEL: It's complicated.

ROSS: Complicated how?

RACHEL: I was born here.

ROSS: You were born here. And before that?

RACHEL: Before that I wasn't born.

ROSS: Your parents came to this country?

RACHEL: Yes.

ROSS: Why?

RACHEL: Because of the war.

ROSS: Because of a war.

RACHEL: Yes.

ROSS: And how does that make you feel?

RACHEL: I don't know. *(Quietly.)* Grateful?

ROSS: Grateful. Grateful how?

RACHEL: What do you do you want me to do… some sort of dance?

ROSS: There's no need to get upset. *(ROSS takes out a marker pen.)*
I want to show you something.

ROSS draws 忠, the Chinese character for loyalty. He shows RACHEL.

ROSS: See this? Do you know what this is?

RACHEL: No.

ROSS: This is the Chinese character for loyalty.
The upper part of the character represents the middle or the centre.
The lower part of the character represents the heart.
The heart is anchored around the centre.
To be loyal is to be steadfast, unchanging, true.
To tribe, to family to country.
Do you follow me?

RACHEL shrugs.

ROSS draws 惡, the Cantonese character for evil.

ROSS: Now this? This is the Chinese character for malevolence, for evil.
Two centres. The heart is uprooted. It has no fixed abode.
The ancient Chinese seemed to think that this caused people to
become two-faced, depraved.

RACHEL: What are you trying to say?

ROSS: Do you like this country?

RACHEL: … Yes?

ROSS: But you don't think of yourself as strictly from here.
Your words not mine.

RACHEL: I said it was complicated.

ROSS shows RACHEL the postcard of the wildcats.

ROSS: Do you practice any religion?

RACHEL: No.

ROSS: None at all…?

RACHEL: No. Why? Do you suspect me of practising a particular
religion?

ROSS: Do you have any deeply held spiritual beliefs that affect your
world-view?

RACHEL: What?

ROSS: Like Wicca? Tai Chi? Homeopathy…?

RACHEL: *(Beat.)* I don't know what you want me to say.

ROSS: I'm just trying to understand. You're not religious. You don't have
a so-called spiritual practice. So how do you explain things?

RACHEL: That's not a straightforward question.

ROSS: Seems clear to me.

RACHEL: I have no idea how to answer that.

ROSS: Here is a table.
There is the light.
Outside it is probably raining.
What is your explanation for all of this?

RACHEL: Can you give me an example?

Silence, until EMMA who can't bear it any more, bursts through the door.

EMMA: 15000 billion years ago, a great fireball of infinite density and heat exploded into a hot, chaotic particle soup. A chunk of it came to be known as planet earth, where some godforsaken accident brought forth the existence of life. Then it was the survival of the fittest. We had dinosaurs, cavemen, dodo birds-which eventually brought about the Wright Brothers. Sooner or later Whitney Houston was singing her heart out on a runway and then you went and bought a toy plastic chicken at the market, which my colleague and I mistook for something more sinister. Now we are all sat here in a holding room Edinburgh Airport, trying to come to some sort of understanding. There's an example.

RACHEL: I would more or less agree with that.

ROSS: So… I'll put science.

RACHEL: Sure. Science.

ROSS: Good. I'll make note of that for the report.

ROSS writes 'science' on a bit of paper.

That's all for now.

RACHEL: Before you go.

ROSS: Yes.

RACHEL: What's your name?

ROSS: My name's Ross.

RACHEL: Your full name. *(Silence.)* I'm sure I have the right to ask you to identify yourself.

ROSS: For what purpose?

RACHEL: In case I need to file a complaint.

ROSS: … Ross Henderson.

RACHEL: And your colleague? The scientist?

ROSS: Emma. Emma Donnelly.

RACHEL: Thank you.

ROSS stands. Stops. Exits the interrogation room. Taking the chicken with him.

FOUR

ROSS enters back into the assessment room with EMMA. RACHEL is alone in the interrogation room.

EMMA: Fuckfuckfuckfuckfuckfuckfuck.

ROSS: It's going to be okay.

EMMA: It's not going to be okay, Ross. She's going to file a complaint. There's going to be inquiry. We're completely fucked.

ROSS: *(A bit panicked.)* Emma. Trust me. It's going to be fine.

EMMA: Honestly. Today of all days. Fuck's sake. *(EMMA goes to light a cigarette.)*

ROSS: What are you doing?

EMMA: We're sacked. May as well embrace it.

ROSS snatches the cigarette away from her and gives her his e-cig.

ROSS: We're not gonna be sacked. I'll think of something. *(Searching-thinking hard. Eureka!)* I've got it! She nuked a live chicken.

EMMA: So?

ROSS: We've got her.

EMMA: She was eight. She did something a bit weird.

ROSS: Doesnae matter. It's clear evidence of an 'underlying psychological tendency towards deviance or the glorification of violence'.

She threatens to move and we pre-emptively counter-strike. We escalate from a Code 3 to a Code 5. Complaint Filed on a Code 3 is looked into. Complaint filed under a Code 5 we get the benefit of the doubt.

EMMA: What's the difference between a Code 3 and a Code 5?

ROSS: Nothing. Nothing, really. Except one of us would have to – You would have to – *(ROSS is aware he is asking a lot of EMMA.)* The protocol calls for a full body search.

EMMA: Nah. No chance. Not doing it. *(Goes to light the cigarette again. ROSS snatches it away.)* I hated that in simulation. I'll probably hate it even more in real life. Not today. Of all days.

ROSS: Emma, please.

EMMA: No chance.

ROSS: Emma, this job is all I've got. My folks would be heartbroken. I'd have to move back to East Kilbride. *(Silence.)* Please Emma.

EMMA: Fuck my life. Just this once.

ROSS impulsively hugs and kisses EMMA. EMMA laughs.

ROSS: I love you!

EMMA: Right, okay. Back off. By the way. I found your perfect outfit.

EMMA holds up the sexy underwear for ROSS. She is wearing a pair of disposable latex gloves.

EMMA: Totally your style. … Very kinky.

ROSS: See that? That's no just kinky. That's deviant. Wardrobe choices reflect evidence of social deviance. Also going in the report. I told you. We're laughing.

EMMA: So far we've got: sexy underwear, wildlife photography and a plastic chicken. This report is going to be class.

ROSS: It will be by the time I'm done with it.

EMMA: How do you even wear this? *(EMMA throws the underwear over ROSS to mock-up how it's worn.)* I think that that goes there…

ROSS: Watch it! This is a clean uniform.

EMMA: Shit.

ROSS: … What?

EMMA: It's just that I remember reading that you can catch genital warts through a canvas uniform. *(ROSS begins to panic.)* I think the warts just burrow through the fabric and implant themselves on your …

EMMA whistles suggesting genitalia. ROSS yanks the underwear off of himself.

EMMA: Now you've just gone and touched it with your bare hands. Imagine how many penises you've just fondled. The warts have spread to your hands… Can you feel them popping up already?

ROSS: I'm gonna need to be sterilized. Where the fucks the sterilizing spray?

EMMA: Oh. I dinnae think we have any uh, sterilizing spray.

ROSS: What's it called the stuff we have?

EMMA: Hand sanitizing gel.

ROSS: Where is it?

EMMA: I've got some here.

EMMA holds a bottle of hand gel close. ROSS attempts to grab the hand sanitizer out of EMMA's hands. EMMA is too quick for him. She breaks away, and squirts a big splodge of it onto his top.

ROSS: That looks… unprofessional.

EMMA: I see my little outfit has had the desired effect.

ROSS: I look like a knob. *(EMMA attempts to clean off his top with a wet-wipe, makes it worse. Laughs.)* You cannae actually get an STI through a uniform can you?

EMMA: For a moment there I forgot how miserable I was.

ROSS: I miss hanging out with you.

EMMA: Yeah. Me too. I mean. You know what I mean.

ROSS: Emma. Look. Since I met you I've been waiting for the right moment. The perfect moment. Maybe you're right. Maybe there is no such thing as the perfect moment. *(Motions to his stained top.)*

EMMA: Ross...

ROSS: – But I've wanted you to know that... Emma, I think you're brilliant. I also. Well.

EMMA: – Ross –

ROSS: – See I have this recurring daydream where you and I are on shift together and I dunno what happens but there's this this moment, right where we both just look at each other. And you say. "Let's get out of here. Let's blow this shanty town". And we run off and find Dan or someone and blag our way on to some training flight going anywhere. Puerto Rico. Mississippi. Bratislava. Anywhere. I'd squeeze your hand as the plane lifts off and together we blast through all the muck and faff our tiny little lives. Past the horizon. Onto something pure. Something real. Emma, I dunno, maybe it's crazy, but I think that together. We could –

EMMA: – It's just –

ROSS: – Emma I've been meaning to say, I'm in love with you.

EMMA: – Ross. *(Silence.)* Please...just... not today.

ROSS: ... No bother, Emma. I'm sorry.

EMMA: It's all right. Just. Not today. *(EMMA hands ROSS RACHEL's phone.)* Here… why don't you run that? I'll finish the writing up.

They sit in silence. EMMA finishes scrawling a section of the report. She looks over at ROSS, who scans RACHEL's phone on a monitor.

EMMA: … Well. Anything interesting in her phone?

ROSS: Well, Aye. I'm just reading through a pretty heated discussion here.

EMMA: What about?

ROSS: Definitely Code 5.

EMMA: On where?

ROSS: … An on-line forum. *(EMMA comes over.)*

EMMA: Seriously. Trip-Advisor?

ROSS: There's been a bit of a mix-up about a spa voucher.

EMMA: A Spa Voucher. Tell me that's not going in the report.

ROSS: "Passion fuelled bust-up in the comments section of an online forum."

EMMA: Wait till I get MI-5 on the line. C'mon. Let's wrap this up.

ROSS: Something doesn't quite add up.

EMMA: What, has she got library fines?

ROSS: There's literally nothing here about these friend-s she's supposedly meeting in Istanbul. Look.

EMMA: Hmm.

ROSS: I mean, for someone like her you would expect to see plans for day trips and toenail colours.

EMMA: Maybe her friends are old? Maybe her friends are old and they're communicating via telephone.

ROSS: Aye. But if they were old, she would have booked their tickets for them. No evidence of that either.

EMMA: Maybe it's a lover?

ROSS: A lover she doesn't email?

EMMA: Let me have a go. Maybe she's got another email? Keep all the embarrassing stuff out of your main e-mail account. Aha!! There. This one.

ROSS: Go to messages. Now we're talking. What have we got here...? Love match. Looks like she's made a friend.

EMMA: He's pretty good looking. *(ROSS looks annoyed.)* I'll run a background check.

ROSS: What's all this? Woah! Nudie selfies!!

ROSS uncovers a series of sexy images that RACHEL has sent to her lover online.

EMMA: Wow. Hello! So that's what she does with all that kinky lingerie...

ROSS flushes. He quickly shuts the window.

EMMA: What did you do that for?

ROSS: That's probably enough.

EMMA: Things were just getting interesting!

ROSS: We've seen what we needed to see.

EMMA: What are you... some sort of gentleman all of a sudden? Or just a prude?

ROSS: I'm just trying to be respectful –

EMMA: – What, do you fancy her, Ross?

ROSS: What?! No. Of course not. I'm just trying to be professional –

EMMA: – Professional. Unbelievable. –

ROSS: – Emma? –

EMMA: – You're a professional. Mackay's a professional. You're all a bunch of bloody professionals.

ROSS: … I'm sorry? I don't understand, Emma.

EMMA: Just. Never mind. You're all right, Ross.

Smiles, a moment.

ROSS: *(Pause, attempts to lighten the mood.)* … Where did you get the perfume from, Emma? You don't have to say. Just it's playing on my mind.

EMMA: – Mackays.

ROSS: Oh. *(Beat.)* Did you stay at his last night then?

EMMA: Aye. I mean. It's not what you think. It was in the bathroom. Must be some bird he's… *(Silence.)*

ROSS: No bother. To be honest, I like your normal perfume better.

The computer that was running the background check beeps. ROSS goes over to read the screen.

ROSS: Well, would you look at that.

ROSS puts the phone in a bag and exits the assessment room. EMMA stays behind to read the monitor more thoroughly.

FIVE

ROSS enters the interrogation room with RACHEL.

RACHEL: Why am I still here?

ROSS: The events of this morning gave us some cause for concern.

RACHEL: I have built a life around trying not to be a cause for concern.

ROSS: I dunno. You got awfully worked up about that Spa voucher.

RACHEL: The hotel was clearly in violation of their own policy. They weren't playing by the rules.

ROSS: And you play by the rules?

RACHEL: I play by the rules.

ROSS: You play by the rules. You're in the game. But you don't feel like you're part of the team. Why?

RACHEL: You really want to ask me that now?

ROSS: You came in carrying a device that looks like a −

RACHEL: *(Sudden realization.)* You went through my photos. *(EMMA enters the interrogation room.)*

EMMA: It's standard practice.

ROSS: We're all professionals.… There's no need to feel embarrassed.

RACHEL: Oh my God.

EMMA: Just because you're sexually liberated doesnae mean you're not a potential terrorist.

RACHEL spits in EMMA's face. For a moment all are shocked.

RACHEL: … I'm sorry.

ROSS: That's it. I'm calling for back-up. *(EMMA reaches for a wet-wipe.)*

EMMA: No. *(EMMA physically stops ROSS from calling for back-up.)*

ROSS: We're escalating this.

EMMA: I said No. Continue your questioning.

EMMA calmly wipes her face. She attempts to turn away. As she wipes her make-up away, she reveals a deep purple bruise beneath her eye.

RACHEL: What's happened to your face?

EMMA: I tripped and I fell.

ROSS: Emma, can I see you next door a second?

EMMA: *(EMMA calmly takes a compact out of her back pocket and re-touches her make-up.)* No. Please. Continue. Your. Questioning.

ROSS: *(Reluctantly turning to RACHEL.)* Now I asked you. Very clearly. At the screening counter. If you were going to Istanbul to meet a friend or friend-s. You said...?

RACHEL: ... Friends.

ROSS: Now is that true?

RACHEL is silent. ROSS places the bagged phone down in the middle of the table.

ROSS: See you can tell me all the sweet little lies you want.
But this wee gadget here. It can tell me more about you than you can ever tell me about yourself. Because it knows you better than you even know yourself. Every whim, every impulse, every insecurity. Now, you're probably wondering why we even bothered having the wee chat we had earlier. Glad you asked. Just a formality. The computer does all the real work. *(Beat.)* So do you want to tell me who you are meeting in Istanbul?

RACHEL: I thought you already knew.

ROSS: Aye I already know. But I want you to tell me. *(Beat.)* Who are you planning to meet in Istanbul?

RACHEL: Someone I met on-line.

ROSS: Someone you met on-line?

RACHEL: A man. I'm going to Istanbul to go on a river-boat cruise with a man I met on a dating website.

ROSS: So just to be clear. You're not going to Istanbul to meet your pals. You're going to meet a man. That you met on a dating website.

RACHEL: … Is that a crime?

ROSS: You lied to me.

RACHEL: … I didn't think it was important.

ROSS: Do you not think that the security of this country is important?

RACHEL: Of course I do I just didn't think it mattered whether. –

ROSS: – What do you know about this man?

RACHEL: He lives in Paris. He makes furniture.

ROSS: He lives in Paris. But he's not properly from there, is he?

RACHEL: He said he's half Iranian.

ROSS: See I took the liberty of running a background check. I take it you didn't.

RACHEL: ? No.

ROSS: But you decided to go on holiday with him?

RACHEL: He seemed kind.

ROSS: It sounds to me like you may have let your emotions impair your rational judgement.

RACHEL: Is *that* a crime?

ROSS: It's not a crime. But it's the precursor to all the crimes.

RACHEL: I still don't understand what I'm doing here.

EMMA: You're here because you lied to a member of security services. Because you're going to an Islamic country. To meet someone who our computer thinks could be open or prone to radicalisation.

RACHEL: What?

ROSS: Do you think she's surprised, Emma? Or do you think she's pretending to be surprised?

EMMA: What do you know about this man's political persuasions?

RACHEL: What did he do?

EMMA: Did he ever talk to you about his political opinions?

RACHEL: No. You've probably seen every conversation we've ever had. We talked about furniture.

ROSS: You talked about furniture.

RACHEL: Yes.

ROSS: I'll be honest. Furniture is a fairly lame topic of conversation.

RACHEL: I liked his coffee tables.

ROSS: Now were you talking about furniture? Or were you speaking in code?

RACHEL: Code?

ROSS: Perhaps coffee table means Vienna? And desk lamp means bomb?

RACHEL: That's ridiculous.

ROSS: But it's possible.

RACHEL: Can you tell me what he's done?

ROSS: *(Simultaneous with EMMA below.)* I'm afraid that's confidential.

EMMA: *(Simultaneous with ROSS above.)* He wrote a newspaper article.

EMMA and ROSS look at each other.

EMMA: Ten years ago, he wrote an editorial in his university newspaper advocating for a ban on the publication of cartoons depicting religious figures. The article caused… a bit of a stir.

RACHEL: It sounds like he just… expressed an opinion.

ROSS: An opinion opposing the freedom of speech?!

EMMA: Just to clarify. He was flagged, not tagged.

RACHEL and ROSS begin to speak in raised voices.

ROSS: Free speech is a fundamental Western Value.

RACHEL: Democracy is based on challenging other people's opinions.

EMMA: Wait a second. Neither of you have actually read the article. Or were actually there.

RACHEL: / People have the right to share their opinion. That's the whole point of free speech/

EMMA: /Can everyone please not speak at once/

ROSS: /At the end of the day someone has to pick up the tab for all these liberal values, and it probably won't be you/

EMMA: – That's enough! You're both giving me a headache.

RACHEL: *(Tearing up.)* Look. When I said coffee table, I meant coffee table. I like coffee tables.

ROSS: That's all for now. *(ROSS and EMMA exit to the next room.)*

SIX

EMMA: It's just an algorithm. The computer tags loads of people. Plus that happened a decade ago and he's clearly not –

ROSS: – What happened to your face Emma?

EMMA: … I tripped and fell.

ROSS: I'm no daft.

EMMA goes to light a cigarette. ROSS takes it away and gives her his e-cigarette again. She takes a few drags. Next door, RACHEL slumps down into the chair, buries her head in her hands and begins to cry. EMMA watches on.

EMMA: No no. Please don't. *(EMMA places her hand on the glass, upset.)* God, I feel horrific.

ROSS: Do you want to tell me what happened to your face, Em?

EMMA: *(EMMA watches RACHEL through the glass, broken.)* It started at the Christmas party.

ROSS: That night. I thought we were having a pretty good time.

EMMA: We were.

ROSS: But then you just disappeared…

EMMA: I went outside for some fresh air. … I'm sorry.

ROSS: You dinnae need to be sorry… I just wondered what happened to you.

EMMA: I ran into Mackay when I was out there. He was stood out there under a lamppost, that had a silver tinsel angel up the top of it. The angel. That's actually the last thing I remember. Until I woke up at his the next morning. I know… you and I … we'd had a moment. But I'd gone and fucked it. What was the point? I thought I'd just add the whole episode to my list of things never to do again. But I kept seeing Mackay at work. He'd never make eye contact. God knows what happened that night. I binned my outfit from that night. Shoes and all. So I didn't have to see it each time I opened my closet. … Then. I dunno, I somehow got the daft idea to confront him about it. This being the age of rah rah feminism and all. So, last night, I went over to Mackay's. He'd been on the drink. In a total state. All. You know that way he gets. But I thought I'd confront him anyway. I'd come this far. I asked if he remembered the Christmas party. I said I couldnae mind any of it, and I just wanted him to know. That was all. But something turns in him. And he kicks off. All of a sudden, he's calling me all sorts. I try and leave but he blocks my exit. When I try and slip past, he pushes me, and I trip and fall head-first into the shelving unit. The whole thing comes crashing down behind me. He says I should stay, we need to talk. He pops two Tramadol into his mouth, washes it down with lager. Says it helps him relax. Come to bed he says we can clean all this up later. And I'm too scared to say no.

ROSS: – ... Emma.

EMMA: But I get lucky. I get lucky. Coz we get to his bed and he immediately falls asleep. But his massive right arm is draped around me and I'm scared to move. So I stay there. And lie awake. At half four in the morning he rolls over the other side, snoring. I take my chance to slip away. He looked so vulnerable, lying there sleeping. all curled up in a ball. I should've just smothered him to death with a pillow.
After that, I had an hour to kill. So I went and sat in a cafe. Had a link roll and a white coffee. Then I came here. And all I really wanted for today was a nice, easy shift.

ROSS: Emma. I'm sorry. I dinnae know what to say.

EMMA: There's nothing to say. *(Shrugs, picks up a plastic tray.)* I've got work to do.

ROSS: You don't have to do this.

EMMA: Let's just get it done with, eh?

SEVEN

EMMA enters the interrogation room.

EMMA: I'm sorry. I know these things can be a bit traumatic.

RACHEL: Can you tell me what I'm doing here?

EMMA: An alert was raised and we are following through as per protocol.

RACHEL: It's all a bunch of Protocols. Policies. Procedures.

EMMA: Can I get you a glass of water?

RACHEL doesn't reply. EMMA pours a glass of water for RACHEL and passes it over to her. RACHEL accepts it and takes a drink.

RACHEL: Thank you.

EMMA: You're welcome. This will all be over soon and we can get you on your way.

RACHEL: What happens now?

EMMA: Well, I've got a few more questions for you.
But first, as a matter of procedure I'm going to need to ask you to remove all items of clothing and place them into this plastic tray.

RACHEL: I'm sorry?

EMMA hands RACHEL a box. RACHEL doesn't accept it. EMMA sets the box down on the table and unfolds a standing screen. EMMA attempts to hand RACHEL a plastic packet.

EMMA: You may change your underpants into this disposable pair. *(RACHEL does not accept the packet.)* You may do so behind this folding screen in order to protect your dignity.

RACHEL: *(Whispers.)* No.

EMMA sets it down in the box on the table.

EMMA: *(EMMA glances over at ROSS, heavy-hearted.)* You are currently being detained under Schedule 7 of the Terrorism Act. Failure to comply with the proceedings may result in –.

RACHEL: You've said. You've already said that. You don't honestly think that I'm a… *(EMMA is attempting to disguise her own discomfort.)*

EMMA: Failure to comply with proceedings under Schedule 7 may result in imprisonment, a fine, or both.

RACHEL kicks the table and shouts, to let out some frustration.

EMMA: We have a zero-tolerance policy for assault against staff and/ or damage to airport property.

EMMA hands RACHEL the box for her clothes. RACHEL stands. She eventually accepts the box. EMMA moves the screen so that it is between them. She turns to face away.

EMMA: Please let me know when you are finished undressing.

RACHEL stands still. The screen covers her mid-section. She undresses herself, meticulously placing her clothes in the tray provided. She opens the plastic packet and dons the disposable underpants. She folds the packet and places it neatly in the tray.

RACHEL: *(Fighting back tears.)* I'm finished.

RACHEL hands EMMA her neatly folded garments. EMMA examines them. Tokenistic.

RACHEL: Do you enjoy your work?

EMMA doesn't respond. She moves the screen away. RACHEL crosses her arms across her breasts.

EMMA: Please hold your arms out to the sides like so.

EMMA demonstrates holding her arms out to the sides. RACHEL obeys and uncrosses her arms. EMMA takes out an electronic device in the shape of a wand and runs it along RACHEL's head and arms, her chest and torso, along her back and down her legs. EMMA runs the wand all the way up the inside of RACHEL's leg. RACHEL flinches. The wand produces no sound.

EMMA: That's all. We're finished. Your clothes.

They hold each other's gaze. RACHEL accepts the tray. She re-dresses.

EMMA: Now, I'm going to need to ask you a few more questions.

RACHEL: *(Silence.)*

EMMA: Is everything okay with your family?

RACHEL: Fine, thanks. Kind of you to ask.

EMMA: Are there any tensions or divisive issues…?

RACHEL: No.

EMMA: Fine. *(Pauses.)* Have you ever been a victim or perpetrator of domestic abuse?

RACHEL: *(Silence.)* No. *(Beat.)* Have you?

EMMA: Failure to co-operate with this investigation can result in imprisonment, a fine or both.

RACHEL: You've said that quite a few times already. *(Silence.)* *(Softly.)* Do you have any more questions for me?

RACHEL looks EMMA directly in the eye. They hold each other's gaze, until EMMA breaks away.

EMMA: No. That's all for now.

EIGHT

EMMA enters the assessment room. She slumps down.

ROSS: I'm sorry. Let's just get her out of here.

RACHEL smashes her first down on the toy chicken.

ROSS: What the hell?

EMMA: Just leave her.

A mechanical twitch, the chicken suddenly self-automates. It speaks to RACHEL in a computer-generated voice.

CHICKEN: Malfunction. Malfunction. *(Beat.)* Ouch. That. Hurt.

ROSS and EMMA cannot hear THE CHICKEN. They are baffled by RACHEL's reactions to it, and assume she is traumatized or going mad.

RACHEL: *(Gasps. Silently points.)*

RACHEL looks over to the double-sided glass. Looks back at the chicken.

EMMA: What is she doing??

ROSS pops his head into the door of the interrogation room.

ROSS: Everything okay?

RACHEL: It's just… The chicken!

ROSS: Aye, it's a chicken.

RACHEL: It's… alive!!

ROSS: Aye… We've seen it laid eggs and that. It's very life-like.
(Beat.) Look. Are you okay?

RACHEL: *(Composes herself, she doesn't trust ROSS.)* Yeah, I'm fine.

ROSS: Are you sure? You seem a bit –

RACHEL: – No it's fine. *(Beat.)* I'm fine. I'm totally fine.
You can go now.

ROSS: … Okay. *(ROSS re-enters the assessment room.)*

ROSS: That was weird.

CHICKEN: Hello.

RACHEL: *(To herself.)* I'm losing my mind.

EMMA: We've actually gone and traumatized her. She's gone mad.
Fuck my life.

ROSS: Look we just need to get this paperwork done so we can get her
out of here as fast as possible. *(RACHEL begins to cry.)*

ROSS: It's fine. Look. She's just having a cry.

CHICKEN: That's it. Let it out.

EMMA: She probably just needs to let it out.

CHICKEN: It's. Okay.

RACHEL: It's not okay… I'm talking to a toy chicken.

EMMA: She's completely fucking lost the plot. *(Pops her head into the interrogation room, replies to RACHEL.)* Hi hun. You okay? *(RACHEL does not respond.)* We're just getting you're paperwork together and then we're going to let you get on your way. Okay? Not long now.

RACHEL ignores EMMA, continues staring straight ahead. At a loss, EMMA returns next door.

RACHEL: *(To the CHICKEN.)* What do you want from me?

EMMA: No history of being sectioned.

ROSS: We just need to get her out of here.

EMMA: I'll call for a porter. *(Speaking into a into WALKIE TALKIE.)* Come in head office. This is Bravo.

WALKIE TALKIE: *(Beep!)* This is Head office.

EMMA: Team Bravo have completed Code 5 proceedings following this mornings incident in Zone 24. No further abnormalities. Our intention is to dismiss the subject and have her escorted onto her scheduled flight for 15h00.

WALKIE TALKIE: *(Beep!)* Copy that. I'll send a porter to Zone 3 in T minus five minutes. Over and out.

CHICKEN: I know how you must be feeling.

RACHEL: No, I really don't think you do.

CHICKEN: You feel degraded. *(RACHEL shrugs.)* I am a chicken. I know what it's like to feel degraded.

RACHEL: Well, what are you suggesting I do about it?

CHICKEN: *(Plays the song from opening.)* Sorry. Malfunction.

RACHEL: I can't sit here anymore.

CHICKEN: Then don't sit. Malfunction. Goodbye.

RACHEL: Goodbye chicken.

CHICKEN: I like your headphones, by the way.

> *The CHICKEN 'dies'.*
>
> *RACHEL feels around her neck, realizes her headphones are still there.*
>
> *She stands.*
>
> *She puts her headphones on. Music.*
>
> *RACHEL nods along to the music.*
>
> *EMMA pops his head into the door of the interrogation room.*

EMMA: Everything okay?

RACHEL: Uh huh.

EMMA: You can sit down.

RACHEL: I'm happy standing.

EMMA: I'd rather you sat down.

RACHEL: Why?

EMMA: It's unnerving.

RACHEL: But it's not a crime.

EMMA: … No. It's not a crime.

> *RACHEL shrugs. A pause. EMMA turns, returning to the assessment room.*
> *RACHEL hates being told to do anything. Especially sit still. She darts a toe out.*
> *Draws it back in. She decides to refuse to be a victim. She's not going to go on*

holiday all mangled and torn. She will dance it out. Right here in the interrogation room. A series of movement builds as the music builds. She dances. Perhaps on the table. ROSS and EMMA watch on. They find it weird, but also strangely liberating. MUSIC ends. Breathing room.

NINE

EMMA and ROSS enter the interrogation room with RACHEL.

ROSS: Everything okay in here?

RACHEL: Absolutely fine. Can I go now?

ROSS: Is, uh, dancing something you do often?

RACHEL: Only in custody.

ROSS: My colleague and I have decided to override the remainder of the protocol so that you may be able to catch your flight.

EMMA: There's a porter on his way.

RACHEL: I'd like to file a complaint.

ROSS: Do you want to catch this plane or not?

RACHEL: I want you to tell me how I can file a complaint. And then I want to catch my flight.

EMMA: *(To RACHEL.)* I'll get you the paperwork.

EMMA exits to get the paperwork from the assessment room. A loud knock on the door.

PORTER: *(Offstage.)* Passenger for Istanbul?

ROSS: Aye!

EMMA: You're free to go.

RACHEL: I'd like to apologize for spitting in your face earlier.

EMMA: I deserved it. *(RACHEL exits.)*

ROSS: Well, if she didn't want to blow up the airport before, she probably does now.

EMMA: I hate this place. I really do.

ROSS: Do you ever think… Maybe this isn't the right job for you?

EMMA: Sometimes I get so bored sitting at that desk I can hear the sound of my own brain cells whimpering and dying.

ROSS: Maybe you need to do something else. You could do anything you wanted.

The sound of an SMS. EMMA gets a text message.

EMMA: That's Mackay. Says he's sorry for last night. Says I should go round later so he can apologize. Says he's bought a roast chicken.

ROSS: I could go with you. Work night out.

EMMA: Nah.

ROSS: What are you gonna do?

EMMA: Get out of here. *(Not with you.)*

ROSS: Puerto Rico. Mississippi. Bratislava…

Blackout.

The End.

CHIC MURRAY:
A FUNNY PLACE FOR A WINDOW

Stuart Hepburn

To Douglas and Annabelle

Stuart Hepburn has been acting, writing and directing plays and screenplays for the past thirty-five years. *Chic* is his sixth stage play. He has written for TV Series such as *Taggart*, *Hamish MacBeth* and *Katie Morag*, and has written two feature films.

Chic Murray: A Funny Place for a Window was first performed at at Òran Mór as part of A Play, a Pie and a Pint on Monday 14 April 2018.

Directed by Stuart Hepburn

Cast: Dave Anderson, Kate Donnelly & Brian James O'Sullivan

It was revived on Monday, 25 March, 2019 as part of the 500 Play Celebration Season

Directed by Stuart Hepburn

Cast: Dave Anderson, Maureen Carr & Brian James O'Sullivan

Foreword

On 29 January 1985, sixty-five-year-old comedian Chic Murray took the last journey of his life. He travelled by car from London to stay at his estranged wife Maidie's house in Edinburgh. He had told her he had something he needed to say to her. He arrived too late to see her and spent the night in the next door neighbour's spare room. He died in his sleep without them having spoken. This is a dramatised account of the great man's last hours on earth.

All of it is true.

Some of it might have even happened.

Stuart Hepburn, May 2020

Int. theatrical space – night.

Blackout.

A piano with a bentwood chair sits stage right. A sofa sits upstage centre. Behind it a stained-glass arch.

SFX 'Nobody's Darling' on the accordion.

MAIDIE walks on with a box of memorabilia and sits on the sofa. She starts leafing through some as the lights come up.

MAIDIE: About five o' clock that morning…I woke up…I don't know why but I opened up this old box of memories… 'Nellie and The Whin Hillbillies'. …'Carnoustie'… 'The Tall Droll and The Small Doll' …happy days…

She sees a specific photo of them both.

MAIDIE: A wee lost boy, and a wee lost girl.

She picks up some sheet music.

MAIDIE: Come lay by my side little darling

Come lay your cool hand on my brow.

Promise me….that you will always be……that you will always… be Nobody's darling but mine…

When I was four I remember my Dad took me to see 'Arthur Tracey'. Yank – big star – this would be the early thirties. Edinburgh Empire. I was already a seasoned professional by then 'Maidie the Wonder Child'.

Tracey's signature number was…

Arthur Tracey strides forward playing 'Marta'.

SFX 'Marta'

TRACEY: Marta, rambling rose of the wild wood.

Marta, with your fragrance divine.

Marta, when I look for your lovelight,

I awake with a sigh,

Then I find you alone.

MAIDIE: He accompanied himself on an accordion – nothing too fancy but plaintive. I looked at that accordion…and I just fell in love with it…so my dad spent his last penny on a half size Hohner and I taught myself. I don't play a fancy accordion……

SFX 'Nobody's Darling' introspective.
She goes back to her memorabilia….as TRACEY crosses over SR.

MAIDIE: You're as sweet as the flowers of springtime
You're as pure as the dew from the rose
And I'd rather be somebody's darlin'
Than a poor boy that nobody knows……than a poor boy that nobody knows…

She sits in reverie.

Lights up on CHIC DSR as he walks on stage carrying a suitcase.

He turns back looks down at an imaginary dog and looks down…

CHIC: Woof Woof. What are you doing following me you stupid hound? Away you go home…woof…woof…don't you bark at me you mangy cur. Away you go home…Woof… Stop that! *(To audience.)* So there I was standing, outside the house talking to this dog…when a man opened the window in his dressing gown…I thought aye aye…that's a funny place for a window.

CHIC's nextdoor neighbour BOB appears. He is wearing a dressing gown.

BOB: What the hell time of night do you call this?

CHIC: I was hoping you might tell me…Wooof…home…HOME!

BOB: In the name of God is that you Chic? What are you up to with a dog?

CHIC: It's been following me all the way from the BBC Club in Botanic Crescent. *(To AUDIENCE.)* I wouldn't mind but we're in Edinburgh.

BOB: What's its name?

CHIC: I haven't asked. I don't want to get too close. It's foaming at the mouth!

BOB: What?

CHIC: Aye I'm having it put down.

BOB: What is it mad?

CHIC: Well it's not pleased! Woof. I told you, GO AWAY!

BOB: What are you doing here anyway? I thought you were in London.

CHIC: I've just travelled up. I want to speak to Maidie.

BOB: Is everything alright?

CHIC: It's personal…I just need to talk to her.

BOB: Have you chapped the door?

CHIC: The place is in darkness.

BOB: She'll be asleep. It's past half twelve!

CHIC: Could I bunk up at your place till the morning?

BOB: Of course, Chic…hang on…

BOB appears and lets CHIC in.

BOB: I seen you on the telly last night… 'Tarby and Friends'.

CHIC: That's a small subset is it not?

BOB: And thon fella with the big nose.

CHIC: Barry Manilow?

BOB: That's the one. Did you tell him the joke?

CHIC: What joke?

BOB: The one about the Blackpool Wedding. You know it.

CHIC: I do not.

BOB: You do so! ... the Blackpool wedding and the woman with the big/

CHIC: HOW DARE YOU ASK ME TO ACCOMPANY YOU TO A PUBLIC TOILET SIR. On the streets of my own country? On the doorstep of my own dear wife?

BOB: Ex-wife.

CHIC: Whatever. Begone! And take your foul practices with you! I'll hear no more of wedding jokes!

BOB: I love that joke.

CHIC: Everybody loves that joke. Except me. I am sick to death of that bloody joke.

BOB: OK, OK, keep your bunnet on...you're shivering, Chic.

CHIC: I've just passed a brass monkey out there with a welding torch.

BOB: Come away in...you're not looking too well at all.

CHIC: Ach I'll be fine.

BOB: I'll get you a wee dram...You can spend the night in the spare room and see Maidie in the morning. You'll be just a few feet away from her here through the wall...

CHIC sits down on the sofa, two feet from MAIDIE.

CHIC: Ach you're a hero Jimmy. *(To AUDIENCE.)* I called him Jimmy. Just to put him at his ease, you know. It's kinna casual but at the same time I didn't want appear too distant. James is a bit formal. It's also a bit strange. Because his name's Bob.

LX cross fade to MAIDIE.

MAIDIE: By the time I was twenty-one I'd worked the length and breadth of the land with the likes of Max Miller, Will Fyfe and Harry Lauder. I was a soubrette with a sideline in impersonation and Buck Dancing.

SFX 'Silvery Moon.'
MAIDIE does a tap dance to 'Silvery Moon'.

MAIDIE: And in the summer of 1943 I signed an eight week contract at the Empire Theatre Greenock. I got off the train. Bucketing. No digs. At the stage door I was told to make my way to 21 Bank Street and 'a Mrs Murray' would sort me out. By the time I got there I was drookit wet and exhausted with carrying my accordion and suitcase up the hill. I was in no mood for comedy.

She knocks on the door with her shoes.

SFX 'Waiting on the Robert E Lee'

Young CHIC and NELLIE are playing Piano and Tea-chest Bass.

NELLIE/CHIC: One Two Three Four!
Way down on the levee in old Alabamy.
There's daddy and mammy, there's Efran and Sammy
On a moonlight night you can find them all
While they are waiting the banjos are syncopating
What's that they're saying, what's that they're saying.

SFX BANG BANG BANG BANG on the door.

CHIC: Mother would you get that?

CHIC/NELLIE: Two three four…Watch them shuffle along
See them shuffle along
Oh take your best gal real pal go down to the levee

SFX BANG BANG BANG BANG ON THE DOOR.

CHIC: Mother, the door!

CHIC/NELLIE: And again…Two three and…Join the shuffling throng
Hear the music and song
It's simply great, mate waiting on the levee
Waiting for the..

SFX BANG BANG BANG BANG ON THE DOOR…

CHIC/NELLIE: …Robert E in the name of Christ mother would you get the door!

CHIC gives up and barges to the door and opens it. And there, standing like a drowned rat with her theatrical trunk and Accordion case is the small but perfectly formed twenty-one-year-old Soubrette, MAIDIE DICKSON.

MAIDIE: I'm looking for Mrs Murray's house…I was told she knew where I could get theatrical digs.

CHIC: No no no no no. There's no digs here.

MAIDIE: There's not much music either. What was that you were playing?

CHIC just stares in silence. NELLIE takes over.

NELLIE: Waiting for the Robert E. Lee.

MAIDIE: You'll be waiting a while then. Your banjo's out of tune.

NELLIE: Who the hell are you?

MAIDIE: I'm Maidie Dickson! And who the hell are you?

NELLIE: I'm Nellie.

MAIDIE: Ever thought of taking up the trumpet, Nellie?

NELLIE: We're rehearsing?

MAIDIE: Need all the rehearsing you can get.

NELLIE: We've got a gig three weeks on Tuesday.

MAIDIE: What is it a Co-Op Purvey?

NELLIE: We're 'The Whinhill Billies!'

MAIDIE: Oh aye?

NELLIE: We're a legend in wur own lunchtime.

MAIDIE: Did your faither meet a musician once?

NELLIE: I haven't got a faither.

MAIDIE: Well did your mother meet a musician then?

NELLIE: I havenae got a mother.

MAIDIE: You havenae got a mother or a faither? What are you?

NELLIE: I'm the Lodger's Wean to my Auntie.

MAIDIE: Oh aye very good and who's this yin?

NELLIE: This is Charles Thomas McKinnon Murray. Better known as Chic.

MAIDIE: Chic? What like in Chicken?

NELLIE: Naw Chic…like in… 'Chic.'

MAIDIE: Has he not got a tongue in his heid?

NELLIE: You usually canny stop him. Chic…Chic…are you alright?

CHIC stares at MAIDIE… and says nothing.

MAIDIE: He's no' the full shilling.

Suddenly CHIC gasps in horror and surveys the scene.

CHIC: Look at the state of this place. Call for Mrs Pollack! Call for Mrs Pollack!

MAIDIE: Who's Mrs Pollack?

NELLIE: Nobody knows.

MAIDIE: This is a mad hoose!

NELLIE: Tell me something I don't know.

CHIC: Nellie away and take a long walk over a short pier.

NELLIE: Whit?

CHIC: Beat it!

NELLIE goes. MAIDIE and CHIC observe one another.
He takes her hand and kisses it.

CHIC: Enchente, madamoiselle. Tell me, what position do you take on the diatonic/chromatic debate?

MAIDIE: Excuse me?

CHIC: The great accordion stushie…keyboard versus button…You do you play the accordion, don't you? Or is that case there just a prop?

MAIDIE: I could play you and Lon Chainey Junior there off the stage!

NELLIE: Ho!

CHIC: Prove it!

MAIDIE: Come and see me. I'm at The Empire for the next eight weeks.

CHIC is well impressed.

CHIC/NELLIE: The Empire?

MAIDIE: …if you DARE…Chic.

MAIDIE leaves. CHIC turns to NELLIE.

CHIC: My mother's put her in the upstairs bedroom.

NELLIE: What about your train set?

CHIC: She's put that in the attic!

NELLIE: But where will we play with it?

CHIC: I've got other fish to fry, Nellie…I'm going to see Maidie at the Empire tonight.

NELLIE: What about our rehearsal?

CHIC: To hell with that!

CHIC takes the stage and dreams…

CHIC: I sat down in the front row of the stalls. She lit up the entire stage. You couldn't take your eyes off her.

NELLIE: YOU couldn't take your eyes off her!

CHIC: She could dance, she could sing she could play she could do everything.

NELLIE: She cannae play the piano!

MAIDIE: That night after the show, I let him have a wee kiss in the lobby.

CHIC: Is that where it was?

MAIDIE: Then he serenaded me on the organ as I lay upstairs…

CHIC: Maestro give me an arapeggio in the scale of D.

SFX 'Two Lovers Down a Coalmine.'

NELLIE on the piano, CHIC serenading.

CHIC: Two lovers went strolling down a coal mine.
The Girl had been a female from her birth.
Give me back the ring I never gave you,
For this is your second time on earth.
Ten weary years have passed in fifteen minutes.
So wipe the cobwebs from your ears.

NELLIE/CHIC: And always think of m-o-t-h-e-r,
And the Dublin Fusiliers.

CHIC salutes and is about to leave.

NELLIE: Where are you off to now?

CHIC: I'm away to see Maidie in Motherwell.

NELLIE: Chic you've been following her about like a collie dug for the last three months! What about the band?

CHIC: The band? The BAND????? She's forgotten more about show business than the pair of us put together.

MAIDIE appears on stage.

MAIDIE: Aberdeen to Kirkcaldy. Ayr to Stranraer... there he'd be... sitting in the stalls staring up at me with that daft looking face of his.

CHIC: I hardly missed a show.

They both go upstage and sit on the sofa.

MAIDIE: The truth was, we were both smitten. One night after a wet Friday in Falkirk, I'm reading the notices and he says to me, bold as brass.

CHIC: Tell me. What do you think about mixed marriage?

MAIDIE: What like Edinburgh and Glasgow?

CHIC: No...no...I mean like you...and me.

MAIDIE: We're not mixed.

CHIC: Well my mother is a Cherokee Indian.

MAIDIE: She's a what?

MAIDIE looks up from the paper.

CHIC: Oh aye full blooded Cherokee from South Eastern Tennessee.

MAIDIE: How did she end up in Greenock?

CHIC: My father met her in Whitby. She had come across with Buffalo Bill.

MAIDIE: Her name's Isabella!

CHIC: Ah but her birth name is 'Tayanita'.

MAIDIE: Tayanita?

CHIC: Aye. In the Cherokee tongue it means 'Beautiful Young Beaver.'

She hits him with the newspaper.

NELLIE: Two years later they were married at St Giles.

SFX Wedding March as CHIC and MAIDIE pose for the camera.

LX Flash.

NELLIE: Chic tell us the one about the Blackpool wedding.

CHIC: I've told you…I HATE the one about the Blackpool wedding!

MAIDIE: Aye well tell them the one about your own wedding then!

NELLIE: His shoes squeaked.

CHIC: Indeed they did not. It was the FLOOR boards.

SFX Squeak Squeak Squeak.

NELLIE: You're going to have to do something about those shoes!

SFX Squeak Squeak Squeak Squeak

CHIC: These are brand new size 11 brogues. I got them with my Uncle Alex's clothing coupons.

SFX Squeak Squeak Squeak Squeak Squeak.

NELLIE: You're walking about like a cross between Little Tich and Wilson Kepple and Betty.

SFX Squeak Squeak Squeak Squeak Squeak.Squeak

CHIC: Maybe I could put that in our act!

NELLIE: Two three four…

CHIC walks the walk as NELLIE cranks up 'Sweet Georgia Brown' on accordion.

Each time CHIC wants to talk, the music goes on…finally he stops the music.

CHIC: Hey…hey…woah……Half of that would have done me. Skedaddle!

CHIC sits at the piano and plays a slow air on the keyboard.

MAIDIE: On our wedding night my Auntie Marion let us stay in her lovely wee house in Dundee.

CHIC: She'd a harmonium in the front room.

MAIDIE: I'd bought this beautiful pink chiffon negligee.

CHIC: Absolutely gorgeous it was… A Mason and Hamlin from Boston, USA. It was polished that shiny you could have shaved in it. I didn't, but you could have done.

MAIDIE: 19 and 6 from Goldbergs…and I'd these lovely Japanese silk embroidered slippers…I went upstairs and got myself looking lovely.

CHIC: Of all musical instruments, on account of its uniformly sustained vibrancy and tolerably distinct combinational tones, the harmonium is particularly susceptible to inaccuracies of intonation.

MAIDIE: I'd got a wee bottle of this Elizabeth Arden scent as a wedding present from Chic's mum…I even put on some Max Factor 'Military Red' … and there I was … resplendent.

CHIC: Who could resist fingering such a wonderful instrument.

CHIC stops playing.

MAIDIE: By the time he had finished playing and come upstairs, I was fast asleep. That was my first night of married life.

NELLIE plays 'Swannee' with CHIC on the piano.

CHIC/ NELLIE: Swannee, how I love ya how I love ya,
My dear old Swannee.
I'd give the world to be,
Back with the folks in D I X I
Even though my mammy's waiting for me praying for me
Down by the Swannee,
The folks abroad will see me no more,
When I get to that Swannee shore.

CHIC: Have you met my wife? She's a redhead. No hair. Just a red head.

CHIC/ NELLIE: Swannee, Swannee, I'm going back to Swannee
Swannee Swannee,
Back with the old folks at home.

As they vamp.

MAIDIE: A few weeks later I was appearing at a charity 'do'. I heard they were short of a musical act. It was in The Usher Hall.

NELLIE is horror struck and stops playing.

NELLIE: The Usher Hall?

CHIC: Aye what's wrong with that? Is it not big enough for you?

NELLIE: Chic we're a semi-pro musical act with a joanna and a box.

CHIC: Not at all.

NELLIE: We do Masonics, Tea Dances and the odd Newton Mearns Bar Mitzvah…this is 5,000 folk at the Usher Hall!

CHIC: Aye but it's Edinburgh. Half of them wouldn't know a six eight if it jumped up and bit them on the arse. What's the matter with you?

NELLIE: My arse is making buttons here you're as cool as a cucumber.

CHIC: Can you not take something for those mixed metaphors?

NELLIE: I can't do it, Chic!

CHIC: You've GOT to do it. It's for charity! Think of those starving weans in Africa…is my bunnet on straight?

NELLIE fixes CHIC's cap. Then decides.

NELLIE: Alright, alright…I'll do it…but no acting the goat between numbers!

CHIC: What do you mean?

NELLIE: You know damn fine what I mean. I'm playing the box and you're standing up the back mooning and telling gags and getting laughs.

CHIC: What's wrong with getting laughs? We're here to entertain the punters…

NELLIE: We're here to play music!

CHIC: Scout's Honour!

NELLIE: So what does he do right after Swanny?

CHIC: So I went into the pet shop and asked the man 'How much are your wasps?' He said 'We don't sell wasps.' I said 'Well you've got one in the window.'

NELLIE: Chic. You promised me you wouldn't!

CHIC: Relax!

NELLIE: Relax? RELAX? Because of your antics I got hit on the head with the safety curtain. The SAFETY CURTAIN! I'm rolling around the stage with the arse hanging out my trousers.

CHIC: Now who's milking the laughs?

NELLIE: That's it! That's my last gig in showbiz, Chic.

CHIC: What are you on about? It was great fun.

NELLIE: For you maybe…I've had it.

CHIC: I need you, Nellie…I don't want to do it on my own.

NELLIE: You need something, Chic, but it's not me…besides…you've got responsibilities.

MAIDIE is thrown a babe in arms.

SFX Slide Whistle POP

MAIDIE: Look at this gorgeous wee boy.

CHIC: Poor soul. He's got his faither's looks and his mother's brains.

MAIDIE: He's gorgeous.

As MAIDIE nurses the baby, CHIC stands for a couple of beats looking bored.

CHIC: How long does it take for them to talk?

MAIDIE: Why?

CHIC: I could do with a bit of company.

MAIDIE: You're jealous!

CHIC: Jealous? Me? Heaven forfend.

MAIDIE: You were an only child. Your mother doted on you. You've been the centre of attention your entire life. This one's put your nose out of joint.

CHIC: My nose?

NELLIE: Gawn, Chic tell them the one about the Blackpool Wedding.

CHIC: Would you shut up about the Blackpool Wedding!

MAIDIE: Shoosh you'll wake Douglas up.
Ally bally ally bally bee.
Sitting on your mammy's knee.
Greetin fur a wee bawbee.
Tae buy some Coulters candy...

She settles DOUGLAS down and sits on the sofa...silence.

CHIC: Anyway you're wrong.

MAIDIE: What about?

CHIC: About me being an only child.

MAIDIE: Oh what's this? Another one like your mother being a Cherokee Indian?

CHIC: I wasn't an only child.

MAIDIE: Charles Murray if you are 'at it' so help me/

CHIC: My mother and father lost a baby the year before I was born.

MAIDIE: They lost a baby?

CHIC: A wee girl.

Silence.

MAIDIE: Have you been speaking to my mother?

CHIC: What?

MAIDIE: Has my mother told you anything?

CHIC: I've not seen your mother in weeks. What are you on about?

MAIDIE: My mum and dad lost a baby too, Chic…before I was born. A wee boy.

CHIC: A wee lost boy.

MAIDIE: And a wee lost girl.

They hold hands.

I've always felt…

CHIC: Lonely?

MAIDIE: No…not lonely.

CHIC: I felt lonely.

MAIDIE: I felt…unfinished. Like there was something…missing.

CHIC: Do you still feel that way?

MAIDIE: No…not now, Chic. Not now.

MAIDIE sits back and changes tack. This is business.

MAIDIE: You know I've been thinking.

CHIC: No good will come of that, you mark my words!

MAIDIE: How about you and me doubling up?

CHIC: Well I have got half an hour before the back shift.

MAIDIE: On stage! A double act.

CHIC: Calm yourself woman. I'm not in your league.

MAIDIE: I could start off with an opening number on the accordion… you could come in and harmonise…we'd do a wee dance… then finish off with a good song.

CHIC: You can do that on your own.

MAIDIE: You can yodel…you could do a few gags.

CHIC: About what?

MAIDIE: I don't know. You never stop telling gags. Life. This and that.

CHIC: This and that? These are things of which I know very little…in fact I was at the doctors the other day and this fellow sat next to me and said 'What do you make of this?' I said 'I don't think much of that.' …In fact, I thought if he comes out with a bag of toffees, I'm off!

MAIDIE: Would you be serious for once. You'd be great.

CHIC: But what about Kincaids? It's regular money.

MAIDIE: Chic. I've been on the boards for the past eighteen years. You've got the talent. You can do this!

CHIC: I don't know.

MAIDIE: I'll help you…Look at this…next week I'm playing 'The Links Pavilion', Carnoustie.

CHIC: Carsnootie? They wash and blow dry their milk bottles up there.

MAIDIE: You and me…what do you say?

CHIC: Let me think about it.

MAIDIE: We could do the Jimmy Davis number and then three gags… alright?

CHIC: What if they don't laugh?

MAIDIE: You've been the funniest man in the room since the day you were born.

CHIC: This is different. This is professional. Professional gags.

MAIDIE: You could do 'The Policeman's Wife!'

CHIC: 'The Policeman's Wife?'

MAIDIE: And errr… 'The Bowlegged Oven.'

CHIC: Do you think?

MAIDIE: AYE!

CHIC: Oh here, I could finish on 'The Lemon!'

MAIDIE: NO! Not 'The Lemon.' Finish on 'The Policeman's Wife.' You finish on the strongest!

CHIC: Right!…Och I don't know…

MAIDIE: Let's try it…come on!

She takes out a notebook and hands it to CHIC.
He takes out a piece of paper with the gags written on them.

MAIDIE: Here…you can write your gags in a notebook.

CHIC: A notebook?

MAIDIE: That's what the big comics do…take it…try…

CHIC: I wouldn't say my wife's a bad cook but we've got the only bow legged oven in the street and I wouldn't say she was ugly but when she sucks a lemon the lemon pulls a face and there was this policeman and he/

MAIDIE: Stop…STOP! What are you doing?

CHIC: I'm telling the gags.

MAIDIE: You've got to give them time to laugh…

CHIC: What?

MAIDIE: Give them time to laugh at the end of joke… 'I wouldn't say my wife's a bad cook, but we've the only bow legged oven in the street.' HA HA.

CHIC makes a note on the paper.

CHIC: Right…

MAIDIE: I wouldn't say my wife was ugly, but when she sucks a lemon, the lemon makes a face.

CHIC: Ha Ha…Yes…I've cracked it!

The MANAGER of the Carnoustie Theatre walks on.

MANAGER: Wait a minute. I never signed a double act. I need a soubrette not a comedian.

MAIDIE: We'll do it for the same money.

MANAGER: What are you on? Ten bob?

MAIDIE: I'm on twelve and six and well you know it!

MANAGER: OK, OK, you can give it a go at the Weds matinee…but if it doesn't come off it's back to 'Marvellous Maidie.'

MAIDIE waits impatiently in the wings.

SFX *We hear the COMEDIAN on stage.*

MAIDIE: Chic…where were you? You're late?

CHIC: Oh I was just in the lavatory polishing up a few more gags.

MAIDIE: More gags? No No…Three gags!

CHIC: AYE. Three gags! 'Bowlegged Oven', 'Lemon' and 'Policeman's Wife.'

MAIDIE: Right…we're on…

SFX robust 'Nobody's Darling'.

MAIDIE followed by CHIC on the stage at Carnoustie.

CHIC/MAIDIE: You're as sweet as the flowers of springtime.

You're as pure as the dew from the rose
And I'd rather be somebody's darlin'
Than a poor boy that nobody knows.

CHIC: I wouldn't say my wife was a bad cook...but we've got the only bow-legged oven the in the street HA HA.

CHIC/MAIDIE: Be nobody's darlin' but mine love
Be honest be faithful be kind
And promise me that you will always be nobody's darlin' but mine.

CHIC: I wouldn't say my wife was ugly, but when she sucks a lemon, the lemon pulls a face! HA HA.

CHIC/MAIDIE: Goodbye, goodbye little darlin'
I'm leaving this cold world behind
So promise me that you will never be nobody's darlin' but mine...

CHIC: This policeman comes home and he finds his wife in bed with three men. He takes off his helmet and says 'Hello Hello Hello.' She says 'What's wrong are you not talking to me?' HA HA.

They end with a flourish.

CHIC/MAIDIE: So promise me that you will never be nobody's darling but mine.

Applause...MAIDIE laughs, bows and walks off.

CHIC stays on stage and bows again.

CHIC: Thank you...thank you...thank you. Actually I got up this morning. I liked to get up in the morning. It gives me the rest of the day to myself.

MAIDIE looks on from the wings aghast.

MAIDIE: Chic?

CHIC: So I got up this morning. Then I got dressed, actually. I always dress. I like to be different but undressed is a bit too different. I went

down the front. You can go down the front to Barry Links there…
there's no law against it.

Silence.

The MANAGER rushes up to join MAIDIE.

MANAGER: What's going on here?

CHIC: …and I was walking in my usual way. One foot in front of the
other. That's the best way. I've tried various methods, I suppose. I
remember once I tried a series of hops. I heard someone say 'Look at
that Australian.' I didn't answer…I just wagged my tail.

MANAGER: What is he up to?

MAIDIE: I don't know!

MANAGER: We're running ten minutes late as it is! I've got Jack Purves
and the Tango Band to get on yet!

CHIC: ……then I met this fellow. I knew him or else I would never have
spoken to him. He was sitting on top of a horse, with a briefcase
bowler hat and Wellington boots. The fellow. Not the horse. I said,
'What are you doing on top of that horse?' He said, 'I thought you'd
ask me that'. HA HA.

Silence.

MANAGER: He's talking nonsense!

CHIC: ……I could have cut my tongue out! I wished I'd never
mentioned it. I thought 'If only I'd never mentioned it. If only I'd just
said "Hello" and never mentioned he was on a horse.' I could have
just passed him by as if it was an everyday occurrence. HA HA.

Silence.

HECKLER: That's rubbish so it is!

CHIC: So I patted the horse. I said, 'This horse has got a flat head'. He
said, 'You're facing the wrong way.'

Silence.

HECKLER: Gerroff!

The MANAGER rushes on.

MANAGER: Right you, OFF!

CHIC: But I haven't finished.

MANAGER: Oh you've finished alright. Strike up the band.

SFX 'No Business Like Showbusiness'.

MAIDIE walks on and drags CHIC off.

CHIC: That went well.

MAIDIE: What on earth was all that about a horse?

CHIC: It was just a wee idea I had…it ends with 'Don't get up on your high horse. HA HA'.

MAIDIE: We said three gags Chic!

CHIC: Half of them loved it.

MAIDIE: The other half hated it!

CHIC: Sometimes you've got to be prepared to lose some to gain some.

The MANAGER struts on in high dudgeon.

MANAGER: I've had six punters demanding their money back. They thought you were shite!

CHIC: Tell them I think very highly of them too.

MANAGER: But I've had twenty new bookings for this evening. Keep it in. And Chic…stop laughing at your own jokes. That's the audience's job!

MAIDIE: And that was the beginning of Chic and Maidie.

MANAGER: 'The Small Doll and The Tall Droll'.

CHIC: I'm a bit worried about the billing. Do you not think it sounds better the other way round? 'The Tall Droll and The Small Doll'?

MAIDIE: Who cares. The small doll is not so small.

CHIC: I thought you were looking a bit peaky…what's the matter?

MAIDIE: What do you think?…I'm pregnant again!

CHIC: Have they found out what's causing it?

MAIDIE: Fine well you know!

Another bundle is thrown on stage.
SFX Slide Whistle POP

CHIC: It's a girl! Now that one does have her mother's looks.

MAIDIE: I'm calling her Annabelle.

CHIC: A wee boy and a wee girl. Our world is complete. There's only one direction for us now…sideways.

MAIDIE: The kids stayed with my mum and dad or Granny Murray, while we made a name for ourselves.

NELLIE marches on with a clipboard in agent mode.

NELLIE: I've got you a grand tour.

MAIDIE: Of what?

NELLIE: Glasgow Corporation Mental Institutions.

CHIC: I've had more fun in a Glasgow Mental Institution than a Blackpool Wedding.

NELLIE: Haw, Chic…tell us the one about/

CHIC: If you mention that wedding once more I will not be responsible for my actions!

MAIDIE: When were you ever responsible for your actions?

CHIC: Actually I was always in charge of my eccentricities!

NELLIE: That was his secret. If Chic was out and about he was 'on'. He was the clown. The funny one. The gigs got bigger and bigger. I've got you the Leith Empire, then it's on to the Edinburgh Palladium then the Cinevariety in Dublin to The Grand Opera Belfast. You're on the crest of a wave!

MAIDIE: Just don't push him too far!

She turns to see CHIC.

MAIDIE: And what are you scratching at?

CHIC: Nothing…it's nothing it's the psoriasis, that's all.

MAIDIE: It's the stress!…I've said it before.

CHIC: Then no doubt you will say it again!

NELLIE: He'll be fine. He revels in it.

She turns on him like a tigress.

MAIDIE: What do you know about it?

NELLIE: Well I /

MAIDIE: Have you the slightest idea the stress of getting up in front of a live audience and making people laugh. Night after night after night?

NELLIE: No, but/

MAIDIE: Well until you do, you keep your thoughts to yourself! You're an agent, Nellie, not a psychiatrist!

NELLIE: Sorry Maidie.

MAIDIE: Och I'm sorry too…I worry about us I worry about him…!

CHIC: I'm just writing out the new routine for Workers' Playtime!

NELLIE: Then its top of the bill with the daddy of them all. Tommy Morgan at the Glasgow Pavilion!

CHIC: I love that man!

MAIDIE: He loves you!

NELLIE: But it wasn't just the stress of life on the road. As the years went on, The Tall Droll's stories grew longer and longer…

MAIDIE: And the Small Doll felt smaller and smaller. Chic could charm the knickers of a peeweet.

NELLIE: The entire chorus line used to stand in the wings to watch his act every single night…

MAIDIE: Aye and didn't he know it!

CHIC: So I was walking down the street and I met my auntie…I said 'Hello, dear' . I call her 'dear' because she's got two horns on her head…anyway I fell into conversation with my auntie about …well when I say 'my auntie' it's not really my auntie…I just say auntie…I mean we've all got that haven't we? Someone we call auntie but isn't……in this case I know for a fact it's not my auntie…it's my uncle.

SFX The accordion starts up and MAIDIE is about to sing but CHIC cuts him off and carries on…

CHIC: So my uncle said to me…if you're passing the butchers get some mince…I said passing? Will I not have to go in? So bold as brass…I set off confidently to the butchers…I like to set off confident. Shows you're a bit of a player, you know. So I was walking down the street… and I fell over…just like that…no no when I think of it it wasn't like that…it wasn't like that at all…it was more like this….so I was lying in the gutter, and this man comes up to me and says…' Did you fall, son? 'I said no I've a bar of toffee in my back pocket and I'm just trying to break it.'

SFX JIG…CHIC and MAIDIE go up to the sofa and sit.

MAIDIE: Chic. Nellie's got us into 'The Prince Of Wales' with Jimmy Wheeler and Mel Torme. Twenty-seven years in this business and I've finally made it to the West End!

CHIC: We were a triumph! Harold Hobson said I was 'Proustian in my depth and Beckettian in my simplicity.' Easy enough for him to say!

MAIDIE: I NEVER want to forget this week. I went to Lyons Corner House for coffee, I had high tea at The Ritz, and seen Buckingham Palace and the Changing of the Guard.

NELLIE: I've got you the big one!

CHIC: Your private life is your affair!

NELLIE: The Royal Command Performance!

MAIDIE: Oh my God. Performing in front of the Queen?

CHIC: Who else is on the bill?

NELLIE: Lee Liberace…

CHIC: Who's he?

MAIDIE: He's a pianist?

SFX LEE LIBERACE'S outrageous, flamboyant 'Nobody's Darling'.

Pause.

CHIC: I'll have to work on my scales…

NELLIE: I wouldn't worry. It's been cancelled.

MAIDIE: Oh no!

MANAGER: The Suez crisis…the Queen won't travel.

CHIC: Liberace was inconsolable. He gret for four hours because he missed out on playing for the Queen.

MAIDIE: I was in tears too! We all ended up back at Winifred Atwell's house getting blitzed on Champagne. After the first three glasses, Liberace stopped greeting. Then Chic sits down at this white Bechstein Grand, cracks his knuckles and asks Winnifred if she plays?

CHIC: She laughed … like a drain. She was lying in the gutter at the time. Then the three of us played boogie woogie till the wee small hours.

The play Boogie Woogie and then NELLIE cuts in.

NELLIE: Liberace's put the word in for you and got you a big American Agent! He's going to take you to the states and break you big style… New York, Broadway, Chat shows, then over to LA. Tinseltown, Movies, the lot. You're going to be an international star.

CHIC: I don't know if I want to be an international star.

NELLIE: Good. Because it's cancelled.

MAIDIE: What?

NELLIE: The American Agent's been killed in a car crash.

CHIC: If I didnae have bad luck I'd have had no luck at all.

NELLIE: Never mind…Francis Ford Coppola wants you for 'The Cotton Club.'

CHIC: A movie? I had enough nonsense with that Casino Royale! I don't want to do another one!

NELLIE: I'm working on a big South African gig.

CHIC: When?

NELLIE: Unconfirmed…In the meantime, I've got you the Bruntsfield Burns Night? No fee.

NELLIE goes.

MAIDIE: Burns Night? We are going to my mother's birthday!

CHIC: But I promised them.

MAIDIE: You promised ME! I never see you these days. They're not even paying you! Are you really going to do it?

CHIC looks at MAIDIE, and then turns to the audience.

CHIC: On a personal note, I'd like to dedicate this Burns poem to an old elocution teacher of mine, Miss Ogilvie, who actually hails from round here…she taught me the poem to enhance my enunciation… and she's in the audience tonight…

SFX Mrs Ogilvie

MRS OGILVIE: Hello there Charles…

CHIC: There she is at the back…I hope I can remember it…I've got an aide memoire here…you might call it a crib sheet…it's called… 'The Cricket Ding by the Old Glay Blick.'
Ye dee when naigs and slaggits doge,
And loo that flaig when niggets baig,
Oh greg and slag when ochits doo will rise awa the griggit.
Oh gravvit grun wi niggets baig,
And loo the same wi nickets dae,
Oh gravit nicket nicked the bag, Aye and slew the flaig o' day.
Ye dee… *(Laughter.)* well, if you are going to snigger there's no sense in me going on…it's difficult enough to remember the words without. *(Clears his throat.)*
Ye dee when lags and liggets dae awa the whooo…oh hurrit whooo… what was that? who hooo…who hoooo …
a liggets day when igget day who hohoooo.
Oh lazz in ay…oh fluck the nigget/no sorry I think I made a mistake there…well it's a while since I did this…hang on.

He repeats it word for word under his breath at twice the speed…

CHIC: Ye dee when naigs and slaggits doge, and loo that flaig when niggets baig, oh greg and slag when ochits doo will rise awa the griggit. Oh gravvit grun wi niggets baig, and loo the same wi nickets dae, oh gravit nicket nicked the bag, aye and slew the flaig o' day. Ye dee when lags and liggets ead awa the whooo…oh hurrit whooo.. who hooo…who hoooo…a liggets day when igget day who hohoooo. Oh lazz in ay…oh fluck the nigget…oh no I'm right enough…I'm right enough… Oh fluck the nigget, dig that blae and grab and grab and carly. Awa with ye in Scots and Picts, arise and fall for Charlie… Thank you and goodnight…

Uproarious laughter and applause.
NELLIE rushes on.

NELLIE: Where the hell have you been Chic? The phone's been ringing off the hook for three days.

CHIC: I walked down from Bruntsfield to see a new show at the Kings and popped into the Green Room at Bennets. That was Wednesday night, I think.

MANAGER: You've got the South African Tour!

CHIC: Oh. I'll go and polish up my Aardvark.

As CHIC leaves SR, MAIDIE enters with the suitcase SL.

She places it on the floor, sits on the sofa, and waits

SFX a car stops, the door slams. A horn peeps and the car goes.

CHIC: *(OOV)* Thanks for the lift.

MAIDIE waits.

CHIC: Maidie….Maidie?

MAIDIE: I'm in here…

CHIC breezes in.

CHIC: Celebration time, sweetheart…We've fixed up the South African tour… JoBurg, Durban, Capetown … number one venues the whole way … telly, radio, the lot … eight grand a week plus all found.

Silence.

CHIC: We'll be living high on the hog…or maybe it's the warthog?… God…what if it's a wildebeest? Living high off the wildebeest…I like that…it has a certain.

MAIDIE is still silent.

CHIC: Would you prefer warthog?

MAIDIE: I know about it.

CHIC: About what?

MAIDIE: I know about all of it.

CHIC: Yes so you keep saying but I'm none the wiser.

MAIDIE: Who just gave you a lift?

CHIC: Just one of the lads.

MAIDIE: For three days?

CHIC: We've been discussing a few new numbers.

MAIDIE: DON'T INSULT MY INTELLIGENCE! It's not the first time. It's not the second time. God strike me down and shame on me it's not even the third time. Why? Why do you do it? It's as if you've got a need to sabotage things…every time things are perfect…you've got to shove your stick in the spokes…

CHIC: Darlin'.

MAIDIE: And don't touch me! … I'm past all that… Do you know, before I married you your mother made me swear I would never leave you?

CHIC: My mother?

MAIDIE: Made me swear it on the Holy Bible… 'don't ever leave my Chic'.

CHIC: She never said that!

MAIDIE: She made me swear on my immortal soul…And for the past twenty years I've supported you, I've driven you, I've cooked for you, I've negotiated the contracts, I've cleaned for you.

CHIC: Call for Mrs Pollack.

MAIDIE: WOULD YOU SHUT UP ABOUT MRS POLLACK!…it's over Chic…I can't do this anymore.

CHIC: Sweetheart.

MAIDIE: I MEAN IT!

CHIC: What will we tell the children?

MAIDIE: As far as I'm concerned it's the pressure of touring…so you just… go to Jo'Burg…you go to Capetown…you live as high off the… hog… as you like…but you go without me. I've had it.

She picks up a suitcase and hands it to him.

He is left alone. NELLIE leans onstage.

NELLIE: Haw Chic…tell us the one about the…

CHIC: Bugger off!

SFX Sad Piano/Gregory's Girl/You'll Never Walk Alone.

CHIC sits disconsolately on the sofa alone.

CHIC: So…I went to South Africa…then New York, Australia…TV Series…cancelled after the first run…Gregory's Girl on the other hand.

We hear the piano tune from 'Gregory's Girl'.

CHIC: 'Off you go, you small boys…' Even played the legendary Bill Shankly…

We hear the strains of 'You'll Never Walk Alone'.

CHIC: When you walk, through a storm, Hold your head up high. And don't, be afraid, of the dark/

SFX cut song

CHIC: I want that played at my funeral.

DOCTOR: It might be sooner than you think.

CHIC: So I went to the doctor, and he said to me 'Take your clothes off', I said 'That's a bit sudden. Couldn't you have asked me out first?' He said 'If I'm to examine you, you'll need to take your clothes off!' I said 'Where will I put them?' He said 'Over there on top of mine'…he said 'What's the matter with you?' I said 'How do I know? That's why I came to see you.' He said 'Oh I HATE it when people come in and say that.'… he said… 'What are the symptoms?' I said 'I've a sharp pain six inches above my head.' …He said 'Tell me, have you had it before?' I said 'yes.' He said 'Well then you've got it again.'

DOCTOR: Mr Murray, this is no joke. You have anaemia and your liver is in dire need of a rest. You need to eat properly, and cut down on the bevvy…capiche?

CHIC: Aye Aye, captain! So I left the doctor's and went for a drink to celebrate…twelve hours later I'm sitting in a cell with a hangover and big Joe Beltrami comes in with the charge sheet.

BELTRAMI: Chic…you're in big trouble here.

CHIC: How do you mean?

BELTRAMI: You were doing sixty mile an hour along Alexandra Parade in a Reliant Scimitar sports car.

CHIC: I was speeding to the sick children's hospital to meet a wee boy that wasn't well.

BELTRAMI: Mmmmhhhh…But you had no insurance, and the car had bald tyres and no MOT.

CHIC: I borrowed it for the day from a friend and I had no idea about any of that legal stuff.

BELTRAMI: Mmmhhh…Chic you'd a blood alcohol count of fifty-one.

CHIC: Ah well you're on your own with that one, Jo, HA HA…but…he got me off…twice. The second time I claimed I was using my car as an office! HA HA

BELTRAMI: Get rid of the car!

CHIC: So…I put the Scimitar up on bricks and carried on!

MAIDIE: Oh he carried on alright. A funny man's never short friends…

CHIC: The deal was they looked after me as long as I told the gags. Everyone's happy…

MAIDIE: Chic the court jester. Chic the clown. Chic the surrealist. But it's a double-edged sword. The minute he drops the bonhommie and the gags he's just that guy with the bunnet wandering up and down Byres Road.

NELLIE: That's not true! People love Chic.

CHIC: Oh they love me alright… 'make us laugh, Chic.' … 'do that one about the toffee in your back pocket, Chic!' … 'tell us the story about The Blackpool Wedding , Chic.'

CHIC is silent. He picks up a phone…
MAIDIE is on her own…

SFX The phone rings three times.

MAIDIE: Hello? … Hello Chic…where are you?

CHIC: I'm in…purgatory is where I am…in hell.

MAIDIE: You can't be in purgatory and hell.

CHIC: I'm in London. I've just done 'Tarby and Friends.'

MAIDIE: I saw you giving Tarbuck the silent treatment on the telly… You were very good…hello? …Hello Chic?

CHIC: I wanted …to apologise for being late.

MAIDIE: You've been late for the past forty years. Why on earth do you want to start apologising now?

CHIC: I've got a lot to say Maidie…I…I…

CHIC is choked with emotion.

MAIDIE: Are you alright Chic?

CHIC: Yes…I'm feeling great…I've never felt better…Can I come and see you up in Edinburgh. Tonight.

MAIDIE: Yes, Chic. Of course.

CHIC: That's wonderful. Wonderful. I'll see you soon.

MAIDIE puts the phone down…and sits back.

LX Return to 'Bob' Lighting state.

BOB: I'll get you a wee dram…You can spend the night in the spare room and see Maidie in the morning. You'll be just a few feet away from here through the wall…

CHIC sits down on the chair.

CHIC: Ach you're a hero Jimmy. *(To AUDIENCE.)* I called him Jimmy. Just to put him at his ease, you know… I know it's kinna casual but at the same time I didn't want appear too distant. COUGH… James is a bit formal. It's also a bit strange. Because his name's emm…… COUGH……his name's…

He sits on the sofa…and stares at the wall, half asleep.

Opposite him, MAIDIE sits looking at her memorabilia.

MAIDIE: About five o' clock that morning…I woke up…I don't know why but I opened up this old box of memories…Nellie And The Whin Hillbillies…Carnoustie… 'The Tall Droll and The Small Doll.' …happy days…a wee lost boy, and a wee lost girl.

NELLIE: Chic!

CHIC wakes up with a start as young NELLIE approaches him.

CHIC: Aye?

NELLIE: I've got a new harmonium.

CHIC: Excellent.

NELLIE: How's your Uncle Alex's brogues?

CHIC: Excuse me …What?

NELLIE: The size elevens you got with clothing coupons?

CHIC: Oh they're…fine…fine…

NELLIE: Tell us the one about the Blackpool Wedding.

CHIC: The what? Sorry who are you?

NELLIE: It's me, Chic…it's Nellie…

CHIC: Oh…for a minute there I thought…where was I?

NELLIE: The Blackpool wedding.

CHIC: Right. How does it go again?

NELLIE: So I went to this wedding in Blackpool. A nice wedding. Well just the usual sort of thing. A man and a woman getting married. Eight times married! Well I didn't know that. But the fellow sitting next to me did. Eight times married he said, in a whisper that carried all over the church.

CHIC: ......in a whisper that carried all over the church. The organist didn't play 'Here comes the bride.' He played 'Here we are again... happy as can be.' ... and an incident occurred there, which I didn't mean to mention. But it's out now...there was...there was...

NELLIE: There was a woman there, who had the longest nose I have ever seen... Now I have nothing against long noses. We have long noses in our family. They run in our family. But she had a real beaut. You could have touched it. I didn't. But you could have. And I thought...if things don't liven up, I will, I'll touch her nose...but what really attracted me to it

CHIC: Really attracted me to it was the way she used it to turn the pages of the hymn sheet. And the cake was brought in. Oh it was a beautiful cake. With candles on it. I said why are there candles on the cake. Someone said 'It's the bride's birthday.' Now I don't know the age of this woman, but the heat was desperate! And...this long nosed woman sat opposite me. And someone, I suppose inadvertently, nodded to her. And she nodded back and cut the cake. The bride was in tears. So was the cake. So we left the hall and made our way down to the tram lines which run in Blackpool. Well THEY don't run in Blackpool. They allow the trams to run in Blackpool. And it was an interesting ceremony, crossing the tram lines. This long-nosed woman was at my back. I knew that because of the constant prodding in my back. At least I was hoping it was her. And she slipped. And as she slipped, she fell. Straight as a dye she fell face downwards, and lodged her nose at the aperture in the line. The line that runs from Fleetwood to erm...erm...well I don't know where it runs I've never been that way. A few of us bent down and took a chance. And we pulled and tugged, but we couldn't dislodge her nose. A heating engineer from Motherwell said 'I think it's the heat of her nose and the cold of the steel that's doing it.' She was frightened. I didn't know that. She whispered from the side of her mouth. Could I be electrocuted? I said 'No. Not unless you throw the other leg over the wire.' ...so instead we took her legs and wheeled her all the way to the depot! HA HA HA.

CHIC laughs uproariously at the joke and sits down and is silent.
LX Return to 'Bob' lighting state.
BOB brings the bentwood chair to the front, walks round to MAIDIE.

BOB: Maidie...I'm sorry.

MAIDIE: What is it Bob?

BOB: Chic arrived last night.

MAIDIE: Where is he?

BOB: He's gone Maidie...He's away.

BOB goes up stage left and off. MAIDIE takes her songsheet out of the box. She stares at the empty chair as a long chord plays.... Finally as the music filters in from the piano, she stands up and walks to the chair, down stage centre.

LX Cross Fade to DSC Special.

MAIDIE: Come lay by my side little darling
Come lay your cool hand on my brow
Promise me that you will always be
Nobody's darling but mine...

...She falters...
CHIC stands up and walks to the back of the chair to support her.

CHIC/MAIDIE: You're as sweet as the flowers of springtime
You're as pure as the dew from the rose
And I'd rather be somebody's darlin'
Than a poor boy that nobody knows.

CHIC pipes up behind her.

CHIC: Anyway after the funeral, I walked out to the garden of remembrance there and there a was a man standing on his own...

about fifty yards away from all the other mourners…the minister said
to me… 'Who's that?' I said 'I think he's a distant relative.'

CHIC/MAIDIE: Be nobody's darling but mine love
Be honest, be faithful be kind.
Promise me that you will always
Be nobody's darling but mine.

CHIC: So I went down the street…down to the front…oh you can go
down to the back…there's no law against it… So I was walking down
to the front… one foot in front of the other…I find that's the best way.

MAIDIE: Goodbye, goodbye little darling
I'm leaving this cold world behind
So promise me that you will never be nobody's darling but mine.

LX Fade to Black.

The End.

IDA TAMSON

Denise Mina

Denise Mina is a novelist, author of the *Garnethill Trilogy* (1998) *Paddy Meehan* novels and the *Alex Morrow* Series. Stand-alones include *Sanctum* (*Deception* in the US), *Conviction* and *The Long Drop*. She has written three original plays: *Ida Tamson, A Drunk Woman Looks at the Thistle* (hour long performance poem), *Meet Me* and an adaptation of Brecht's *Mr Puntila* and *His Man Matti* for a co production between the Traverse, Citizens and Dot Theatre company of Istanbul. Improvised comedy series *Group* was co-written with Annie Griffin and premiered on BBC TV in 2020. Comics include a year long run on *Hellblazer*, an original graphic novel *A Sickness in the Family* and an adaptation of Stieg Larsson's *Millennium Trilogy*. Literary prizes include the CWA Dagger for best first novel, CWA Dagger for short story of the year, the Theakston's Old Peculiar Award in two consecutive years and the 2017 Gordon Burn and MacIlvanney prizes for *The Long Drop*. *Conviction* was a joint winner of the MacIlvanney Prize 2019. *Conviction* was a *New York Times* best seller and a Reese Witherspoon Book Club pick. She has been shortlisted for The Edgar, The CWA historical and short story daggers. She has served as a judge for the CWA, The Womens' Prize for Fiction and the David Cohen Prize.

She has contributed to *The New York Times*, *La Liberation*, *The Guardian* and *The Herald* and presents radio and television documentaries.

Ida Tamson was first performed at at Òran Mór as part of
A Play, A Pie and A Pint on Monday 12 June 2006.

Director: Morag Fullarton

Cast: Elaine C. Smith, Clare Waugh & John Morrison

It was revived on Monday, 10 June, 2019 as part of the
500 Play Celebration Season

Director: Lesley Hart

Cast: Elaine C. Smith, Paul James Corrigan
& Joy McAvoy

SCENE 1.

Interior. Shabby office of *Take-a-Break* magazine.

Back Projection of Take a Break headlines in the TaB font:

>   Sniff Me, I'm as Clean as Whistle
>   Asda Gigolo
>   Boot Sale Tales
>   Death by Tattoo
>   Are You Leaking, Margery?
>   True Secrets: All Letters Are Genuine
>   Dead Grannie's Warning
>   Stop it, Stacey!

A messy magazine office. There is a desk in the middle of the room with two chairs facing each other. On one side of the stage is a small table with a kettle and coffee and biscuits. On the other side is a stack of cardboard boxes.

Enter HELEN, followed by IDA who has an outdoor coat on. HELEN carries a clip board.

IDA's coat is cheap. She carries a Primark plastic bag. She is excited to be in the office.

HELEN is a young journalist who is doing a wages job in a lady's magazine. She is middle class and dressed in a Hobbs suit and high heels. She has a faint tan and bare legs, but the tan isn't orange or obvious.

There is no demographic overlap between these women, no common ground.

HELEN looks as if she knows where the good parties are. She doesn't seem interested in IDA at the start but gradually becomes intrigued.

HELEN: *(Off hand.)* Thanks for coming in.

IDA: *(Excited – looking around.)* Aye, no bother.
Nob'dy'll believe I've been in here.
So this is where the magic happens?

HELEN blanks the comment. IDA is embarrassed.

IDA: I thought ye just came out to the house?

HELEN: Yeah, usually we do, but when you offered, well, I've got a lot of work on and it just saves us the drive.

IDA: Don't know if you could park around my bit anyway.

HELEN: Yeah? Is the parking bad?

IDA: Em, well, no, there's a lot of spaces… Too many, ye might say.

IDA laughs weakly, embarrassed.

IDA: It's a bit rough. Cars tend to go two ways: on fire or just away.

HELEN: Oh, I see: joy riders.

IDA: B.Y.T. Barlanark Young Team. 'Bams in Your Toyota.'

IDA laughs loudly. HELEN smiles, polite but bored. IDA is embarrassed.

Well, that's what we call them anyway. Everyone I know reads it.

HELEN: Reads what?

IDA: *Take a Break.* Everyone I know reads your magazine.

HELEN: *(Smirking.)* Really?

IDA: Why are ye surprised?

HELEN: No, well, we know the circulation's good but, it's just, I don't know anyone who reads it.

IDA is uncomfortable again and HELEN finally makes an effort.

Except my gran. And she doesn't buy it, her buddies give it to her. Well, she bought the last couple of issues, just to see my name printed in the back, in the credits, you know that big list of tiny names next to the competition entry slip?

IDA: The bit you cut out to send in?

HELEN: Yeah, facing the 'tell your story' form.

IDA: I sent that in.

HELEN holds up the clip board and lifts the flimsy slip.

HELEN: Got it.

IDA is pleased to see the familiar slip.

IDA: There it is. I like that, the five questions: 'Who is in this story?', 'What happened next?'

HELEN: You remembered. Well done.

IDA: I've been looking at it for ages, weeks. I didn't know if you would even be interested my story, didn't know if it was interesting enough but then when you phoned, I could hardly believe it.

Looking disinterested, HELEN arranges two chairs facing each other, one down stage, one up. She invites IDA to sit in the chair facing the audience. As she speaks she sounds bored.

HELEN: Oh, it's exactly the sort of story that we're interested in. So… seat?

IDA sits down. She glances at HELEN's legs.

IDA: Been on holiday? You've got a tan.

HELEN: Oh, it's fake tan. Superdrug's own. It's not real.

IDA: Looks just like the real thing, though, eh? Ever try that San Tropez?

HELEN looks at IDA, surprised she knows the brand.

HELEN: Yeah but it's pretty expensive.

IDA: Not at Blochairn. Know the boot sale? Ye can get a gallon of San Tropez for a quid there. Goes on a bit darker though.
What bit of the magazine is the story going in?

HELEN: We're thinking 'A letter from the Heart'.

IDA: *(Very excited.)* On page three? The full page spread?

HELEN is not excited at all. She sits down opposite IDA.

HELEN: Exactly.

IDA: 'Letter from the Heart'. Geeso. I thought it might be one of the Readers' Realities but I never thought it would be a full two page 'Letter'.

Gasps with delight.

Is there – will it be mentioned on the cover?

HELEN: Well, yeah. The Letter usually gets a strap line of its own.

IDA is breathless with excitement.

That's if it is 'A Letter'.

IDA is a little crestfallen.

IDA: I don't mind –

HELEN: It sort of depends on what else is in this issue.

IDA: I don't mind. It doesn't matter. Maybe a big fire'll come in, or a true murder.

HELEN: Yeah, sometimes other people get a big story at the last minute.

IDA: Fine. That's fine. It's not a murder, my story, it's not your fiancé running off with your lesbian mother at your wedding or anything great like that.

HELEN: Tea?

IDA: Only if it's no bother.

HELEN hesitates. She can't be arsed making tea.

HELEN: No, okay, it's not a problem.

She gets back up heavily, puts clip board on the seat, and goes over to the coffee table and puts the kettle on.

Milk? Sugar?

IDA: Milk. Have ye any sweeteners?

HELEN: Oh, somewhere.

Now that HELEN's back is turned, IDA looks tired and frightened. She talks to cover her feelings.

IDA: Lovely. Three please.

Ye give up sugar and then realise that the sweeteners are even sweeter, ye get used to them, know? I wouldn't take sweetener before but now I don't like sugar. It's not sweet enough for me now. Get used to them. Get a taste for them. Sweeteners…

Pause. IDA tries again.

Did you just start working here? Is that how your gran started looking for your name?

HELEN hates this job.

HELEN: Last month.

IDA: Exciting!

HELEN: *(Muted.)* Yeah… exciting.

She delivers the tea to IDA but doesn't take one herself. The tea spoon is still in the mug and IDA negotiates it over the next exchange, trying to drink with it in the cup, taking it out when HELEN isn't looking, searching and failing to find a place on the desk to put it down. Finally she puts it back in her mug and drinks with it in the mug, jabbing herself in the face with the handle rather than be rude.

IDA: Not really?

HELEN: Well, three years studying journalism. *Take a Break* wasn't quite where I saw myself working. Thought I'd walk into the *Guardian* features section.

IDA: Is that different?

HELEN: A bit, yeah.

IDA: Better?

HELEN: No, I don't mean that. But it's different. More in depth. Just, everyone reads the *Guardian*, you know, can have a bigger impact.

IDA: More people read it than read *Take a Break*?

HELEN sounds as if she is repeating a pitch from a sales conference.

133

HELEN: Actually, this magazine's circulation is thirteen times more than the *Guardian*. And those readers are more likely to pass their copy on so I suppose the over all-readership is much higher. But it's a weekly and the *Guardian* is a daily, but if you take the readership into account… in terms of influence…

She looks at IDA and realizes she is talking over IDA's head.

It's a different demographic.

IDA: *(Weakly.)* So I suppose.

HELEN looks at the clip board with the slip on it.

HELEN: So, you're here to tell me about … Mary.

IDA: Yes.

HELEN: You know usually we just go by what's on the slip and a couple of follow up calls but I didn't understand the ending of the story and wanted to ask a couple of questions.

IDA: Fire away. I still live in Barlanark.

HELEN is confused by the interjection but carries on.

HELEN: Mary…

Gets her Dictaphone and snaps it on loudly. IDA looks at it, suddenly uncomfortable. When she talks she leans into it and speaks stiffly.

So your daughter, Mary, died?

IDA: Yes. *(To the tape.)* I still live in Barlanark. I stayed. Never moved. *(To HELEN.)* … Just … because you didn't have the tape on before…

HELEN is again confused.

HELEN: But it says in the form that you later found out that she didn't die and you'd buried the wrong person?

IDA: Oh, yes. Mary wasn't dead. But she probably is again.

HELEN nods to IDA to continue talking but IDA doesn't understand the cue and nods back uncertainly.

HELEN: Why did you think she was dead?

IDA: Well, she was found dead. In the flat. With the baby. Didn't you remember the story from the news?

HELEN: Sorry…

IDA: Mary'd been dead for days… Johnny, the baby, was left alone with her. He was three month old. He was licking damp off the side of his cot.

HELEN obviously doesn't remember but is slightly disgusted by IDA now. IDA senses her disapproval.

HELEN: Yeah, I remember something about that, I think.

IDA: Well, it, the body was all… The heating was high. Mary's methadone prescription was in the pocket and I hadn't seen her for a long time. Her stuff was all over the house.

HELEN nods as she takes this in. IDA is lost in her memories.

I had to go the mortuary and identify her. The man, he pulled the sheet back fast… I couldn't look at … She was red, all swollen from the heat. They said it was her who am I tae…Paid for the funeral myself.
I was hanging around the Tesco discount shelves like a bad smell for months…

IDA hears how she sounds and squirms in her seat.

HELEN: But the body wasn't Mary? It was someone else?

IDA: I'm not doing this for the money.

HELEN: What?

IDA touches her worn coat.

IDA: I need the money, ye can see that, but I could have money if I wanted. That's not why I'm telling you my story.

HELEN: It's all right if you are.

IDA: But I'm not.

HELEN: Two grand isn't to be sniffed at.

IDA smiles and then stops herself.

IDA: Aye. I suppose.

HELEN: So, you identified her body and thought your daughter was dead from an overdose?

IDA: Aye.

HELEN: And then, four years later you heard it wasn't her, she wasn't dead?

IDA forgets her mask after mentioning Barlanark again. She doesn't look at HELEN until the end, and before then her true self comes out.

IDA: Eh, in the post office, one day. I was in the queue, waiting, in Barlanark, where I stay, and then it was my turn so I went up to the window and the lassie was serving me and she says, 'Oh, and I saw your Mary the other day at my cousin's house.' And I was shocked, ye know, and I was like that 'did ye? Ya fucking cow!' Well, I was hurted, ye know, shocked. And she's like, 'I did, I've known her for years and it wiz Mary' and I'm like 'She's been dead for years, Mag'ret Fraser, ya vicious wee shite' and Mag'ret's like that 'Naw 'cause I seen her.' I was bealing! Our youngest, Johnny, he's five, just started school at the time, and that's the last thing he needs to be hearing. I banged on the window a wee bit and she's like *(Holds her head back, shouting over her shoulder.)* 'Security!' Got dragged out. Pulled all the passport forms off the shelf but. Went all o'er.

IDA titters, then realizes she's let her cover slip. She straightens her coat and clears her throat. HELEN is disconcerted. She jots something down on her clip board.

HELEN: Oh. I see. Who was the cousin?

IDA: Oh. *(Lying)* I don't know.

HELEN: You surely know who Margaret Fraser's cousin was? Didn't you go to their house looking for Mary?

IDA: *(Lying.)* No.

HELEN: What did you do then? See this is the problem, Ida, you know the last question on the 'Tell Us Your Story' form? *(Shows IDA the flimsy slip on the clip board.)* The last bit is 'How did the story end?' You hearing that she isn't actually dead, that doesn't feel like an ending.

IDA looks at the clipboard.

IDA: Well, she wasn't dead, that is the end. Now I've got her two kids, two boys. I'm bringing them up in Barlanark, where I stay.

HELEN: Yeah, I saw that on the tell-your- story form. That's why I wanted to talk to you in person. See, in the form she's just sort of around again and that's not really an ending. There's no resolution.

IDA: Um, well, she knew where we were. She could have come to find us, if she wanted to see us. I've never moved. It's the house she grew up in. In Ba–

HELEN: Barlanark. So you keep saying… In Barlanark.
See, Mrs Tamson, I think our readers are going to wonder why you didn't go looking for Mary when you heard she wasn't dead. Most mums would go looking for her, ask her why she put her things in the dead girl's pocket to make it look like her.

IDA: Well, she was hiding. Owed a lot of money I suppose.

HELEN: But then, suddenly, everyone knows she isn't dead and that doesn't seem to matter, there are no consequences. And didn't she want to see her own kids? Didn't you try to see her?
D'you see what I mean? The story doesn't end there.

IDA: Maybe I didn't want to see her.

HELEN: Why?

IDA looks shifty and shrugs.

IDA: I'm … busy.

HELEN: Busy?

IDA: I've got two kids tae raise.

HELEN: Mary's kids. She's in so much trouble that she fakes her own death, leaves her kids and runs away but then she comes back years later for some reason but doesn't come to see them? Why?

IDA: *(Shrugs.)* She wasn't bothered?

HELEN: The story doesn't really make sense to me. See, to be a 'Letter From The Heart' the story really needs to be about something sad happening to people who are quite sympathetic.

IDA: 'Sympathetic' – what does that mean?

HELEN: You know, a nice lady.

IDA: You saying I'm not nice?

HELEN: No, I'm just saying –

IDA: I don't care if ye don't think I'm nice. I don't need you to like me.

HELEN: I didn't say I didn't like ye.

IDA: I see that look all the time, ye know.

HELEN: What look?

IDA: When I telt ye Mary died in the house and the baby was left there. That look. Disgust or whatever it is. I don't give a monkey's. Doesn't even fucking touch me.

Pause. HELEN is shocked at how aggressive IDA is.

Doesn't bother me. They can look at me however they like. I know what I done. She was missing for a year and I was out every day looking for her. I only had my wee Malik, just me and him in the buggy, every day, without even the bus fare, in the pissing rain, in the cold, walking, looking for her.
It wasn't like she was dead next door and I wasn't fucking bothered.

I couldn't find her. *(Crying.)* I was always looking but I couldn't find her.

There wasn't gangs of women gossiping about me at the bus stops then, was there? See, I don't care what they say about me. I know what I done. Choices I made. I know I tried.

HELEN: I'd like to put that in, that you were looking for her before she was found dead. That's good. It makes you likeable.

IDA is upset.

IDA: I don't care what they say. But I've got the boys and they see how people are with me. Spitting at my feet, turning away fae me.
I don't want them… They're only five and nine.
Good boys. I want to protect them from… I mean, Mary saw things, growing up and I regret…

HELEN: Ida –

IDA: I don't want the boys to grow up with people looking at me like that, saying things to them when I'm not there…

HELEN: Ida, when I asked you to come in here –

IDA: I don't mind the looks myself, I can take it, it's them –

HELEN: – I know who you are Ida.

IDA is stunned.

IDA: Who?

HELEN: You. I know who you are.

IDA: No you don't.

HELEN: I do.

IDA gets up to leave, knocking the chair over. HELEN stands up too.

It was the Flesher's cousin, wasn't it? In the Post Office.

IDA pauses with her back to HELEN.

He found Mary and brought her back, didn't he? Held her hostage?
He told Margaret Fraser to tell you so that you'd go and see him,
didn't he? What did he want from you?

IDA turns to her.

IDA: *(Panicked.)* Nothing.

HELEN: Did she owe him money? Is that why she staged her own –

IDA: – He wanted nothing. I've got nothing.

HELEN: Stories can end lots of ways. This isn't the *Washington Post*, we
can tell any story you want to tell.

IDA: Because the real story, I won't... These people –

HELEN: – I know what you've been through. I want to help. Want to get
your story in the magazine.

IDA moves off a little but stops when HELEN speaks again.

The story you want to tell, Ida. Nothing else, not the other stuff. We'll
find an ending.

IDA turns back.

I won't mention King Hogg but they'll know he's your husband, the
people who spit at you.

They'll know you're still in Barlanark, that you didn't move into
Hogg's mansion in Mount Vernon.
That's what you really want to tell them, isn't it? That you haven't
moved, haven't taken his money. Because it's dirty money...

IDA softens a little.

IDA: I could get money if I wanted it.

HELEN: I know you could. I saw you smile when I said two grand was
a lot.

IDA: I won't talk about looking for Mary at the Flesher's house neither. You can't show your weakness...

HELEN: Whatever you want. We'll just say you looked for her when she came back but she didn't want to be found. That you did your best. 'A mother's heart break'. 'My mother- of-a-junkie Hell'. People love that stuff. We'll make you sympathetic... Come back, Ida.

IDA stands tall at the door. She narrows her eyes at HELEN.

IDA: You think you know what I've been through?

Black.

SCENE 2.

Interior. A room in the Flesher's house.

Back projection of a smart West End living room.

This scene takes place before the meeting with HELEN and IDA. It is lighter in tone, IDA is less careworn.

To denote the passage of time: she has the same coat on but it is less frayed. She is carrying a different, less crumpled plastic bag.

All the furnishings are packed for shipment. IDA is lead into the room by JANINE. She is glamorous, posh and elegant. She wears a very narrow pencil skirt.

Cardboard boxes are stacked against one wall. The house is being packed.

JANINE: In here, Mrs. Tamson. I'll let him talk to you himself.

IDA: So Mary was here?

JANINE: I'm sure Peter'd rather speak to you in person about that.

IDA: Peter? Since when was he called that?

JANINE: That's his christened name.

IDA: I thought even his mammy called him 'The Flesher'.

The women stare at each other.

Since when were you on the scene?

JANINE: Peter and I met three years ago. Been inseparable ever since. You're out of touch Mrs Tamson. Doesn't gossip get through the walls of that big Mount Vernon house?

IDA: I wouldn't know what gets through the walls, I don't live there.

JANINE: That's right. He moved and you stayed in that pokey Housing Association flat in Barnlanark. Why did you never divorce King Hogg? You could get a lot of money.

IDA: I don't want that sort of money.

JANINE doesn't understand. She's in it for the money.

JANINE: Has he got a fancy woman in there?

IDA: He's not that kind of man.

JANINE: *(Cynical: she thinks she knows a thing or two.)* All men are 'that kind of man'.

IDA: D'ye think? You're very wise for a wumman wearing a skirt she cannae fucking walk in.

JANINE: So he has got a girlfriend.

IDA: *(Exasperated.)* No, he hasn't. D'you think King Hogg Tamson could have a bird and every wide-o in Glasgow wouldn't know about her? Women – that's your man's weakness. What you need to watch out for.
Ye need to know what their weaknesses are if you're going to work them.

JANINE flinches.

Aye, you should know that. He'll dump ye eventually for another bird, a younger bird, a posher bird or whatever.
Women's the Flesher's weakness…

JANINE is offended.

JANINE: And King Hogg? What's his? Small boys? Girls?

IDA: He's greedy, if ye must know. Greedy for money.

JANINE: Greedy enough to sell heroin to his own daughter?

IDA grabs her by the neck as THE FLESHER comes in.

IDA: How fucking dare you.

THE FLESHER is vain. His eyebrows are over-plucked, he's tanned, wears designer clothes. He really cares about his appearance.

FLESHER: Ida.

IDA: Ya cow –

FLESHER: Ida.

IDA lunges for JANINE. THE FLESHER pulls them apart easily.

Put her down, Mrs. T.

IDA: Some bint out of Glasgow Academy, living in fucking Bearsden all her life –

Respectfully holding IDA by the wrist, he guides her back to her seat.

FLESHER: Leave her, Mrs T. She's not one of us. She doesn't know the rules.

IDA shouts at JANINE.

IDA: He never knew she was taking it out of his stash. He'd have leathered her if he'd known. He's only greedy for money, he's not a murderer.

FLESHER: Well, Mrs T, let's not just lie through our arses now…

IDA and THE FLESHER look at each other and smile.

Ye must stop attacking people. Think you're on 'Real Housewives of Barlanark'?

They laugh. They're fond of each other.

IDA: How are ye, son?

THE FLESHER dismissed JANINE with a flick of his wrist. She leaves.

FLESHER: Not bad.

IDA: Ye look prosperous enough.

THE FLESHER playfully places a hand on his hip.

FLESHER: Does that mean fat?

IDA: No, your threads, ye look nice son, handsome. Ye turn yourself out lovely.

FLESHER: Thanks. I try.

IDA sits back in her seat. THE FLESHER holds up a bottle of Remy Martin XO cognac. It's a fancy bottle.

Drink?

IDA shakes her head and looks at the fancy bottle.

IDA: What kind of drink is that?

FLESHER: XO. Cognac. *(Sees she doesn't understand – patronizingly.)* Brandy, to a mug like you.

IDA watches him pour himself a brandy in a balloon glass and warm it by swirling it in his hand.

IDA: Oh look, a balloon holding a balloon.

THE FLESHER take sit in good part.

FLESHER: *(Smiling speaking as if to a child.)* Don't annoy me now…

He keeps the smile on his lips but glances a warning at her: the ghost of a smile with a scary threat underneath it

IDA: *(Very nervous.)* She here?

THE FLESHER stalls by taking a long sniff of the brandy.

You're a cruel wee shite.

FLESHER: I'm about to answer ye.

IDA: Is she here?

FLESHER: No, Mrs. T, she's not here.
I heard you made quite a spectacle of yourself in the post office.

IDA: *(Snarky.)* Keeping tabs on pensioners' slap-fights in the PO? *(Turns serious.)* Ye told Mag'ret Fraser to pass on that Mary was here, didn't ye?

FLESHER: I did, aye.

IDA: Well, ye got me here.

What is it ye want to tell me? Is she dead or not?

IDA's courage fails her and she looks imploringly at THE FLESHER.

FLESHER: Mary isn't dead. That body you buried – wasn't her. Oh, I'm as surprised as you, believe me. Quite shocked when I heard she was in Manchester working in a meat factory. Been there a few years, apparently.

IDA: You brought her back?

FLESHER: She put up a struggle. Black van outside her work. It was in the *Manchester Evening News.*

Looks at his cigarette again, dragging it out.

IDA: I suppose I've just got tae sit here and let you fucking drag it out as much as ye want.

FLESHER: You're in no position, Mrs. T.

IDA nods.

So, I found her.

IDA: Bring her back to use her against her daddy?

FLESHER:: I wouldn't have gone to all this trouble over King Hogg. He's a spent force.

IDA is surprised.

Aye. Old King, sitting in his big new house, watching the monitors of the drive way tae see who's coming for him.
No one's coming.
No one gives a shit about him anymore. He's not even a player anymore.
(Whispers playfully.) Don't tell him. It'll make him sad.
No, Mary and me... We've got business of our own, Mary and me...
From way back. When she went AWOL I looked for her. She'd been staying with me for a while.

146

IDA: *(Nervous.)* What?

FLESHER: And then one day she just vanished.

IDA: You had her here, like a hostage?

FLESHER: *(Smirking.)* For a while. She was here for the free kit. Why d'ye think King Hogg let me set up on my own?

IDA doesn't quite understand.

IDA: You kept Mary here, feeding her drugs, using her to threaten her father?

FLESHER: At the beginning. But then, well, things developed. Mary's a beautiful woman. I wasn't the only one who thought so. She *was*. She was a beautiful woman.

He pauses to let this sink in.

Sorry. You haven't see her You wouldn't know her. Ye'd walk past her in the street. I looked for her, after she ran. She owed me a lot of coin. Everywhere I went they said 'her mammy's just been here'. You were looking for her too, weren't ye, Ida?

IDA is tearful as she remembers the time.

IDA: I was, aye.

THE FLESHER is enjoying her distress.

FLESHER: Your heart must have been roasted.

IDA gives him an evil look. THE FLESHER kicks her chair.

Don't make me slap ye down, Mrs T. We've always got on.

She gives him the look again.

IDA: Go on, hit a pensioner for looking at ye funny. Big man.

FLESHER: Ye want tae know what happened?

IDA, defeated hangs her head.

IDA: I do, aye.

FLESHER: Not dead. Found her in Manchester. Brung her back.
She owes me... nothing personal. But a man in my position can't
allow a bird tae walk off owing. Rest of the dugs see that...
Then, just as the guys were extracting payment she comes out with it.
There's a wean, she says.
Johnny. He's mine.

IDA is shocked and panicky.

IDA: How could ye know he was?

FLESHER: I didn't know. She knew.

IDA: But you said she was putting it about –

FLESHER: Stop. She's done all that. She's tried the backtracking, Ida,
but I know now, eh?

IDA: *(Sputtering)* Ye moving, are ye? Where are ye off to, not Mount
Vernon, I hope..?

FLESHER: No. Spain.

IDA: Spain? Lovely! Where about?

FLESHER: Malaga.

IDA: *(Almost screams.)* Malaga!?

FLESHER: Aye, d'ye know it?

IDA: No. I've heard about it. Seen it on 'A Place in The Sun'! Nice.
Sunny. When are ye off?

FLESHER: Soon. The boy...

IDA: *(Rambling, speaking very quickly.)* I never went to Spain. See, when
King Hogg went on holiday I just stayed home with Mary, I'm not
bothered about going away. Load of fuss about fuck all if ye ask me.
We get sun here, don't we? I don't even like it when it's sunny here.

Largs. That's a holiday. Nardinis. My pal had a share in a caravan in Girvan. Were ye ever in Girvan?

FLESHER: Girvan's a shite hole

IDA: Aye, it is a bit. But Dunoon –

FLESHER: We can't avoid talking about the boy by working our way up and down the West coast.

IDA: We could try.

FLESHER: The boy. He's my son. I'm taking him to Spain with me.

IDA smirks uncertainly.

All I know is he's called Johnny. What is he, four now?

IDA nods dumbly.

I'm glad it was you that brought him up.

IDA: D'ye think I'm just going to hand him over tae ye?

FLESHER: Mrs. T. You're forgetting something: I've got Mary.

IDA: Mary told ye about Johnny?

FLESHER: Aye.

IDA: Ye were about to kill her and she said 'the wean's yours'? How d'ye know she's not lying?

FLESHER: Regretted it as soon as it was out her mouth but she'd said it. Couldn't take it back.
So, Mrs T., you've got another boy?

She nods again.

A Paki wean?

IDA flinches at the word.

IDA: Malik's Scottish.

FLESHER: But he's a Paki, eh? Got the Paki skin. Don't like that. My John being brung up with a Paki wean.

IDA: Malik's a good boy. Looks after his wee brother.

FLESHER: A Paki looking after my wean? Can't have that…

IDA: You're showing me your hand.

THE FLESHER is suddenly vicious

FLESHER: I don't really give two fucks what you know, Mrs. T. You've got no hand to play. I'm leaving, for Spain. Why am I leaving?

He pauses.

Bits of information, papers, photies send to CID by a certain old man. A redundant, retired old man who's just moved house. Because of your man I need tae go and live in Spain. Can't come back.

IDA: You're taking Johnny to spite King Hogg?

FLESHER: I'm taking what's mine.

IDA: You can't own a wean.

FLESHER: You'll gae him to me.

THE FLESHER takes a photo out of his pocket, looks at it and hands it to IDA. She clamps her hand over her mouth. Stares. Strokes the picture with her finger.

Lost her looks.

IDA tries to speak but is overwhelmed.

You'll give him to me. Are ye listening to me? Ida. *(A play on the phrase 'listen to me when I'm talking to you'.)* Listen tae me when I'm threatening ye.

IDA can't stop looking at the picture.

I'm leaving for Spain early tomorrow. Tonight, I'm coming to your house.

Have him ready.

THE FLESHER grabs her hair and pushes her to the floor.

Woman. Have the wean ready. Seven o'clock tonight outside your close.

He stamps on a corner of her photograph. She tried to tug it free but it rips. He lets go of her.

She is on her knees, holding up the corner in her hand.

IDA: Her face. My baby's face.

Back projection of the ripped, badly focused photo of Mary looking frightened. Her hair is being held to keep her in the shot.

SCENE 3

Interior: Helen's freelance office

Back Projection of article headlines from various publications. Each is in the characteristic typeface of the publication it is from.
Closer: Davina's Custody Hell
Marie Claire: Fat, Fit, fabulous!
Bella: 'Fuming' Louise Speaks Out
Heat: Lose twenty pounds in four weeks

This is a different office. A smaller, less busy office. In this scene IDA is confident and HELEN is obsequious. The dynamic is reversed.

HELEN looks less tidy: she has had a baby since she last saw IDA and is sleep deprived. She is less together and confident.

HELEN: I'm so pleased to see you, Ida.

IDA: Aye, and you.

HELEN: How are the boys?

IDA: Good. Johnny was six yesterday.

HELEN: Lovely. Party?

IDA: Auch, naw, just a spaghetti dinner and a wee sponge. His brother made him a truck out of Lego. He's trucks mad.

HELEN: Out of Lego?

IDA: Red. Put wee windows in it and everything. A bonnet. He's awful clever, our Malik, know? Kind.

HELEN: So, Ida, did you see the *Take a Break* article?

IDA: *(Not very excited.)* I did aye. Letter from The Heart. I look a hundred in that photo.

HELEN: *(Lying)* You looked beautiful.

They look at each other, HELEN a little embarrassed, IDA sceptical.

IDA: This is my best side *(Gestures to the back of her head)*. But they took the photo from there *(Holds a hand up to her face, inches from her nose.)* and it was sunny and windy at the same time so I was like that. *(Makes an ugly face.)* Aye, *(Points to the back of her head.)* with the lights off and heavy fog I could pass for Angelina Jolie.

Sees HELEN laughing and is a little offended.

Hey, I was a honey when I was young. But ye never know that about yourself until you're auld.

HELEN: Did everyone see it? Did it work?

IDA starts cold and gradually warms up, becomes triumphant.

IDA: Worked fine, aye. They started off ignoring me. Normally when I was up the Asda I'd see at least one, looking at me, mouth like a cat's arse. That was the first change I noticed.
(Grinning.) Then it was the teachers at the boys' school.

IDA waves and smiles insincerely.

'Hello there, Mrs Tamson, boys are doing great', lovely lovely, all nicey nicey. The boys see that, the teachers being respectful, giving ye your place.

And Malik stopped acting up in the house. *(Embarrassed and shifty.)*
Not that he ever did, 'cause he's a good boy. But after that he seen me different. It's hard for them. The other mums are young and well, it's just hard for them.

But now everyone knows I never took the money. Fought for their mum and that. Boys are kind of… You know, bit proud of me…

HELEN: I did what I said I would, didn't I? I didn't mention anything you didn't want me to.

IDA looks at her askance.

I didn't though, did I?

IDA: Yeah. Well, you don't get brownie points for not fucking me over.

HELEN: No, I know I'm just saying… I'm glad it worked.

They fall into an uneasy silence. IDA moves around the room.

IDA: And here ye are.

HELEN: *(Smiling.)* Yeah. Freelance isn't secure but it's more fun. One day I'm working on a story for *Bella*, next day for the *Independent*.

IDA: Not the *Guardian*, though?

HELEN: Not yet. Have to find the right story.

IDA: *(Diffident.)* I had a look at that paper after I met ye.

HELEN: Like it?

IDA: Not really. 'S like being shouted at by a social worker.
Why don't they have competitions? Or more pictures?

HELEN: They have some pictures…

IDA: Was your granny disappointed ye left *Take a Break*?

HELEN: *(Very touched and tearful.)* You remembered?

IDA: I'm not an animal, I remember other people have families.

HELEN: No, it's just, it's such a load of old shit. I don't know how she could read it week after week. She used to call me, ask which articles I'd written and I could hear her writing it down so she could tell her pals. Anyway, she passed away.

IDA: Oh, I'm sorry. So … did ye want to see me for the *Bella*?

HELEN: Actually, no. I was hoping… Tea?

IDA: Can ye make tea in here?

HELEN: I can get one from the machine in the hall?

IDA: Nah. Powdered tea, gritty. Gets all stuck under your plate. What is you want, hen?

HELEN: Um, I want to do another interview.

IDA: Ye said that. But not for the *Bella*?

HELEN: No. I wanted to interview you about your background this time.

IDA: *(Flattered.)* My childhood? There's not much to say −

HELEN: No, Ida, your background.

IDA: You want me to talk about him?

HELEN: Ida, this interview, it would be totally anonymous. No pictures and I'd change your name and all the details about you, no one need know it's you.

IDA: But they will.

HELEN: Not if we're clever about it, Ida.

IDA: Stop saying my name all the time. Ye sound like a salesman.

HELEN: They wouldn't know it was you.

IDA: How do you know? You wouldn't know what to cut out or change. The tiniest detail and they'll know it was me. If I mention living with a gangster the polis'll be all over me, they'll think I'm ready to turn.

HELEN: Okay, I don't understand those subtleties, but I could let you read it before it's published. If you say scrap the whole thing, I'd do it.

IDA is wary.

Ida…*(catches herself saying the name)* Sorry. But listen, I want this story to be about you, about Glaswegians who have lost their kids to drugs, the heroes who step in to raise the next generation, how unsupported and unlauded you are. People don't know that stuff.

IDA: *(Steely.)* Auch hen, I've got my own worries.

HELEN: I know you care, you've already taken a stand. You wouldn't take his money. You refused to move.

IDA doesn't answer.

D'you know Scotland has the highest rate of drug deaths in Europe? Doubled in ten years.

IDA: *(Angry.)* Fuck all to do with me. *(But interested.)* I never heard that figure.

HELEN: No one has because the people dying are Mary. *(Angry.)* You heard of the opoid epidemic in America?

IDA: Fentanyl and that? Heard they're dropping like flies over there.

HELEN: Yeah. Drug companies sold it as non-addictive. 'Safe for twelve year olds', it said that on the packet. Prescribed to everyone. Kids with football injuries, middle class kids. It's so addictive that dealers are improving their heroin by cutting with fentanyl. 72,000 deaths from overdoses last year. Now families are suing the manufacturer.

IDA: Quite right.

HELEN: Yeah, it is right. But they only care because it's affecting white, middle-class kids. Not kids in schemes. Not kids like Mary. We have a massacre here every year and no one cares because they're the wrong kind of kids.

IDA shrugs and moves around the room.

Don't you care?

IDA looks at her and crosses her arms.

IDA: This is for the *Guardian*, isn't it? Your big chance to make your mark?

HELEN: *(Shamed.)* How did you know?

IDA turns away.

IDA: 'Cause it's fucking boring. How do I come into it anyway?

HELEN: Don't you think people would be interested to know what it's like, to live with a dealer and lose your daughter to an overdose?

IDA: My daughter didn't die of an overdose. I just thought she did.

HELEN looks through her notes.

HELEN: But she did die because of drugs?

IDA: *(Lying.)* Aye. Yeah, she did.

HELEN: Mary? She is dead, isn't she? Have I got that wrong?

IDA: Well, I don't... know, really. Mibbi.

HELEN looks confused.

HELEN: I thought you cared about all of that.

IDA: *(Angry.)* I care about my own.

HELEN: Really? *(Impersonating IDA.)* Yeah, mibbi Mary's dead, I don't really know. I'm not bothered –

IDA: *(Furious.)* You know nothing. Ye know nothing about me.

HELEN: I want to know. Come on, sit down, Id-

IDA gives her a warning look.

I helped you when you needed it.

IDA: Ye did your job. I'm not a mug. You wrote the story that way because it suited ye. It was a good story –

HELEN: *(Losing control.)* It could have been a better story. I could have taken it and exposed you in the Record. 'Gangland Granny turns on King Hogg'. Could have done that.

IDA: *(Spitefully.)* Too late now. Missed your chance.

HELEN looks tired and, shamefully, tries a final gambit to get IDA to talk.

HELEN: I know how you must feel, as a mother: I've just become a mother myself –

IDA: *(Furious and shocked.)* Don't even fucking try.

HELEN: What?

IDA: Don't even try that as-a-mother shite with me. You sitting up in a some nice house worrying about healthy snacks at the nursery and I've got two wee boys who think ye get to twelve and it's time tae start carrying a hunting knife. You know how I feel. That's a new low, even for a journalist.

HELEN squints at IDA.

HELEN: Oh yeah, I can see the resemblance to Angelina Jolie now...

IDA laughs despite herself. HELEN spots a chink in her defenses.

I'm trying to do some good here. If I can get an emotive story to highlight the failings in the way we value the people dying of overdoses it could have a big impact. It could save lives. Even the police say they can't get coverage of the overdose rate. They're pumping out these statistics and no one wants to cover them until a doctor's son dies.

IDA: Oh, the police, aye? Well, they're right about everything...

HELEN sits back, defeated.

HELEN: Okay, fine, Ida.

IDA gives her a look for saying her name.

Yeah: Ida, Ida, so punch me. Why don't you chuck passport forms all over my office.

IDA goes to leave but pauses at the desk and puts her finger under a pile of papers, tipping them so they slide to the floor. HELEN looks at them lethargically.

(Sarcastic.) Nightmare.

IDA smiles, she likes HELEN's attitude.

Well, I'm going to be up all night, PTSDing this violent episode.

IDA smiles and shrugs a laugh. She takes out her nicotine chewing gum.

IDA: Boy or girl?

HELEN looks tired and does a self-comforting gesture, strokes her hair or something.

HELEN: Boy.

IDA: Weight?

HELEN: Seven seven.

IDA: Good weight.

HELEN: Yeah. He's a handful. *(Tearful.)* When you're pregnant you vow that everything'll be perfect and then you're so tired you lie awake in the night listening to the baby crying, wishing they'd just shut the fuck up.

IDA smiles knowingly.

IDA: He's not sleeping?

HELEN: Not for longer than an hour at time. I feel like I'm being tortured by the CIA.

IDA picks up the spilt papers.

Please talk to me.

IDA: What about?

HELEN: Did you ever see Mary again?

IDA: I saw her. In his car. Outside my house.

HELEN: He brought her to your house?

IDA: Didn't bring her to the house, no. Drove her outside and kept her in the car. I saw her. From two hundred yards away. She saw me. Raised her hand. Smiled a big smile as they drove off, oh, but she was thin…

IDA is lost in the memory.

HELEN: And then he drove her away and you never saw her again?

IDA: That's it.

HELEN: Why the 'big smile'?

IDA: *(Smirking.)* She saw something that made her happy.

HELEN: She saw her boys?

IDA: Both her boys, aye.

HELEN: So he brought her to show her the boys? Why?

IDA: *(Shifty.)* Dunno…

HELEN: Flesher's moved to Spain now hasn't he?

IDA: He's an arse.

HELEN: Was Mary in love with him?

IDA: *(Smirking.)* She faked her own death to get away from him. Not in love with him, no.

HELEN: To stop him coming after her?

IDA: Eh?

HELEN: Was he in love with her?

IDA: I don't think so. Mibbi. Early doors. The Flesher likes a bit of strange. Weak for women. It's one of his big weaknesses.

HELEN: He's got more than one weakness?

IDA spins towards HELEN, suddenly angry.

IDA: You're not going to do that again are ye?

HELEN: What?

IDA: That innocent-but-I-know-what's-going-on thing ye did the last time?

HELEN is surprised by the change in tone.

HELEN: No.

IDA: You. Look at ye. You know things about him. You're at it.

She picks up her bag and moves towards the door. HELEN watches her but IDA stops at the door. She turns slowly.

Not saying anything?

HELEN: I don't know what you expect me to say.
I'm so tired.

IDA turns slowly.

IDA: You don't know anything about Mary, do ye?

HELEN: No, that's why I'm asking you. But you're being so bloody obnoxious, I'm finding it hard to care.

IDA: Okay.

She comes back in, sits down, smiles at HELEN.

HELEN: You said women are the Flesher's weakness.

IDA: One of them.

HELEN: There's more than one?

IDA: He's got two very obvious ones anyway.

HELEN: What's the other one?

IDA pauses.

IDA: Have ye noticed, since Brexit, all the racists are crawling out the walls?

HELEN: He's a racist?

IDA: He said to me he didn't like Johnny being brung up with Malik because he was a Paki. Can ye believe that? Said that word to my face. Malik's daddy was from Bristol.

HELEN: But why would he care how Johnny was being brought up?

IDA: *(Blustering.)* When The Flesher was a wee guy he was never away from my house. I was good to him and then he says that about my boy to my face.

HELEN: Oh my God. The Flesher's Johnny's dad, isn't he?

IDA doesn't answer.

And a man like that wouldn't let a son slip through his fingers. Is that why she ran? Keep Johnny away from him?
They say every man wants a son.

IDA doesn't answer.

IDA: Vain men. That's who want a son.

HELEN: He found out, didn't he? When Mary reappeared.
(Realising.) Is that why he brought Mary? To swap Mary for Johnny? And you chose Johnny.

IDA: No. *(Diffident – she wants to tell but knows she shouldn't.)* I didn't have to choose in the end. He changed his mind at the last minute. He didn't even get out of the car and Mary was smiling because she realized what I'd done…

HELEN: Why didn't he want Johnny?

IDA: Didn't like the look of him.

HELEN: The look of him?

IDA shakes her head and smiles.

IDA: You been on holiday?

HELEN: Why didn't he want him?

IDA: Not been away, naw?

HELEN: *(Confused.)* What didn't he like about Johnny?

IDA: Nice holiday, somewhere sunny, get a wee tan.

HELEN: But Mary was smiling?
She knew the Flesher would kill her but she was smiling..?

IDA: You've got a tan.

HELEN is exasperated.

HELEN: I haven't been on holiday, I've just had a bloody baby, it's fake tan.

IDA smirks.

It's fake tan... The Flesher didn't like the look of him? You covered him in fake tan? He thought Johnny was Asian too?

IDA: That San Tropez, ye can get a gallon of it at the boot sale for a quid. You have to know their weaknesses

HELEN: And Mary was smiling?

IDA: She looked out the window and when she seen both of them the same colour... She looked at me and... a big smile... Respected me. Grateful. She hadn't looked at me like that for a long time... They say, at the end of the day, all ye want is for your weans to love you back but that's not true. All ye want is for them to know how much you love them... She knew... *(Clears her throat.)* I knew what she wanted me to do. He'd tell me himself. *(Imitates THE FLESHER.)* 'tried backtracking, she's tried all that, Mrs. T.' Couldn't stop himself boasting. Weakness blinds ye. All The Flesher could see was the colour of him.

HELEN: What happened to Mary?

IDA: *(Quietly.)* She knew the Flesher'd kill her anyway. Borrowed time. Too many threads left hanging if he didn't. But she saw her boys and she knew they would be safe with me. She smiled...

Pause.

I have to hope I did the right thing by her, saving Johnny.

HELEN: You did. It's what she wanted.

IDA: I hang onto that smile...

HELEN: You did the right thing. No one should be made to chose like that.

IDA: You can't judge me unless you've been in my place. Folk'd think; 'I'll call the cops' – I can't. 'I'll get a gun' – I'd get five years and the boys'd be in care. 'I'll save Mary somehow' but no one could –

HELEN: No. I've never been in your place and I can see it. You did what you could.

IDA looks at HELEN.

IDA: Repeat any of that to a living soul and I'll come to your house when you're sleeping and stab you through the eye with a pencil.

HELEN: If I ever sleep again.

IDA points at her.

IDA: To your grave.

HELEN: To my grave.

IDA sits down and puts her bags on the floor.

HELEN: *(Awed.)* Ida–

IDA: You let me read it before ye put it in the paper?

HELEN: What?

IDA: The interview, the one about the grannies and the working-class kids dying of overdoses?

HELEN: *(Respectful.)* I will, Ida, yeah.

IDA: *(Annoyed.)* Well, get a fucking move on then. Some of us have got homes to go to.

The End.

JOCKY WILSON SAID

Jane Livingstone and Jonathan Cairney

Jane Livingstone wrote her first play, *Thieves of Dunfermline*, in 2014 and has since written four plays for A Play, A Pie and A Pint. She was one of the BBC's Scottish Voices 2019 and is a recipient of a Playwrights' Studio Scotland Partners Award. She also won a Scottish BAFTA New Talent Award for her screenplay *Roses of Picardy*. **Jonathan Cairney** is a teacher, musician and songwriter. He and Jane are siblings and regular collaborators. They are both based in Dunfermline.

Jocky Wilson Said was first performed at at Òran Mór as part of A Play, A Pie and A Pint on Monday 20 March 2017.

It was revived on Monday, 13 May, 2019 as part of the 500 Play Celebration Season

Directed by Tony Cownie

Cast: Grant O'Rourke

SCENE 1 – ONE FOR THE ROAD

The set is in darkness. There is the sound of radio static before we hear a few bars of Van Morrison's Jackie Wilson Said. As it fades out…

RADIO DJ: *(V.O. California accent.)* So it's another beautiful day in California folks, one of the hottest of '79 so far. Hope you're keepin' it locked on WKDY, and, whatever you're doin' today, staaaaay cool…

The radio is switched abruptly off and the lights come up to show a bright, sunlit desert scene. There's a large cactus, a road sign that reads 'Las Vegas 180 miles' and a low, craggy rock.
Through the audience comes a short, stocky man [JOCKY], carrying a small suitcase and wearing an open collared top with 'Jocky Wilson' written on the back. He trudges up to the stage and stands, back to the audience, reading the road sign.

JOCKY: Fuck's sake!

He turns, paces about, wiping sweat from his brow, squinting into the distance.

180 mile?! That means I've only come – what – a couple a miles. In –

He looks at his watch.

– just over an hour! Well that's no bloody use. Got to be on the oche at nine. I'll never make it – unless some bugger stops for me.

He shakes his head.

One more for the road Jocky they said. One more for the bloody road. Now I ken what that means. One more drink and you're hitching to Vegas – on the bloody road right enough.

There is the sound of a distant car engine approaching.

Hud on, hud on, we might be in here!

JOCKY sticks out a thumb to flag the car down. It doesn't stop and JOCKY throws up in his hands in despair. He sits on the rock, placing the suitcase beside him.

JOCKY: Christ these legs weren't made for long distance. I'm no that sort of sporting hero.

He looks at the cactus.

What you looking at pal? Never seen a top athlete stopping for a breather before? Just going to sit here for a bit if it's all right with you like. I'm maybe better staying in one place and waiting for a car to go by.

He takes a cigarette packet out of his pocket and, realising it's empty, throws it to the ground.

Keeps getting worse! Stuck in the middle of nowhere with no fags and no even a wee shop in sight.

He sighs.

See that's the thing about travelling. Talking about it's aye better than doing it. The journeys I like are the ones where I'm heading back home – and that's a fact.

He opens the suitcase.

The rest of the boys will be at the hotel already. Wonder what they're having to eat. I could just go some mince and totties. Or maybe a steak bridie. Och you've got yourself in a right pickle this time Jock.

Pause.

Sun's roasting. Burntisland Highland Games the day – they've got a braw day for it anyway.

SCENE 2 – ORANGEADE

JOCKY: *(Looking into the suitcase.)* Dinnae ken why I bother with this. Just the two pair of underpants in it. Only bring it because it looks good in the airport.

He opens the case and takes out a pair of large pants.

These are my lucky pants tae. Can be tricky getting the timing right – always at their luckiest on the third day's wearing.

He mops his brow with the pants then does a double take at the case interior. He blinks and reaches into it again.

Hell's this?

He takes something out. It's a clear drink in a mini bar style bottle.

Well that's a welcome sight! Cheers, Spike!

He takes a sip, makes a disgusted face and spits it out.

WATER! Hey Spike, I dinnae ken what circumstances a man would have to find himself in to drink that stuff. My gran, she told me the English poisoned the water. That's why I always used to brushed ma teeth,

He smiles a gummy smile,

with orangeade. Best to be on the safe side eh?

People are aye asking how I cope without teeth but I can manage just about anything with my gums. Can chew a steak if it's well done. Can even eat apples. Great Yarmouth rock and nuts are the only things that defeat me. False teeth are useless anyway – 'cept for marking the cue ball at the snooker – they're handy for that.

He looks at the water bottle.

A vodka would just have gone down a treat there as well. Was the vodkas that did for me last night mind. That and the chance to make a few extra bob off the boys in the bar.

Strange playing darts in these big Yank hotels – some settings Sinatra wouldnae have turned his nose up at. But the game's just the same. And it's just as bloody sore when you lose...

That's the thing about darts – you can beat all the top pros and then get gubbed by one of the punters from the crowd – man or woman! Like that cowboy last night. That wasn't his first time at the oche, I can tell you.

SCENE 3 – HUSTLER

JOCKY: *(As a HUSTLER, American accent.)* Man I can not believe I've beaten Jacky Watson, a guy they tell me is gonna be world champ one day!

He turns to address JOCKY.

You may have lost my friend but hey, it's three in the morning and I couldn't even hit the board if I'd shipped as much liquor as you have. Pretty damn impressive.

He holds out his hand as if for money.

Yeah that's what we agreed.

Say, this ain't your last dollar is it? Must have been up about a thousand bucks a few hours back. You were winning plenty against the pros.

JOCKY: My speciality. Here, I've missed my lift. Bobby and the others left hours ago apparently. But I've got a match. Got to get to Vegas. And I've a flight to catch. Home. Is there anybody about here could give me a lift? Any chance you could –

HUSTLER: Give you a ride? To Vegas? You gotta be kidding mister. That's nearly 200 miles! And there's still some night left for me to spend this dough. I don't give a rat's ass if your buddies have left without you. You shoulda gone when they did –
(To himself.) 'stead of hanging round here, getting played.

Guess you got to hit the road Jacky! And by the way – Vegas is that a way.

(To himself.) Man I thought he was gonna take a pop at me then. Little guy sure hates to lose.

SCENE 4 – THE LISTER

JOCKY: Boy was right, eh. I mean I'm all for shaking the hand of the other player, I always make a point of that. But I must admit I dinnae like to lose. No that is not a feeling that's good to have. And I kent that from the very first time I threw an arrow.

1970, Pele and his pals were in Mexico showin' awbody how it should be done. Me, I was in Kirkcaldy, twenty years old and making up the numbers in the Lister bar darts team. It didn't go well…

JOCKY: *(As RAB, strong Fife accent.)* Aw now dinnae greet Jock.

He laughs.

I mean I've been beat but I've never been grannied! That was a total whitewash.

Your first ever game of darts and maybe your last! You'll probably no get close to a dartboard again – not that you were ever close there!

I thought you were supposed to be good at the sports. Were you no the pole vault champion at Waid Academy or something? That's what awbody says.

That you away Jocky? Away to practise? Away to pole vault all the way home?

(Calling after a departing JOCKY.)

Can you even afford a dartboard to practise on Jock? Heard you left the fish factory. Can you no stick at anything, apart fae the brew? See wi' this Jock – you'd be as well gi'in' up before you even start!

SCENE 5 – MOZART

JOCKY: Everyone knows I like a joke, even if it's on me. Always like a bit of patter. I could do wi' some of the friendly faces from the Lister Bar here the now. They look after me. Always did. I got an old dartboard off the guv'nor there and his wife, Mrs Blyth, she used to gie me the money to go to the tournaments.

I did some amount of practice like. Had to. When you're five foot and a dog's end you're punching above your weight. You have to work twice as hard just to hit the board.

See back when I first started with the darts Spike, I practised more on that board than bloody Mozart did on his piano or Karpov at his chess. That's a thing about being on the dole, you've plenty time on your hands. And the practice paid off. Went from the Lister team to the Links team and then it was playing for Fife. Some great players in that Fife team I tell you. Only Scottish team to beat all they English teams. Even beat London. Aye London, with all the top Anglos! And then Spike – one of the proudest days of my life – first cap for Scotland. No disrespect to my opponents like but when I play for my country I'm nigh on unbeatable. I'll be honest, when I first started though I was too nervous, too keen to do well. I used the drink to give me confidence cos I just kent the darts could be something big for me eh, and for the family.

Although there's been times when the drink's cost me matches, like last night. And I hate that. I hate it.

Aye I know when I'm fu' I can be a prickly wee bastard – no offence – a bit of a toerag.

And I can get distracted by the slightest thing eh. Glasses rattling and fruit machines paying out. No like John Lowe. Old Stoneface. That man has elegance. Hundred per cent focused on the shot. Watch him too closely and he'll hypnotise ye. I may hit more 180s than he does but he takes the percentage every time. A master. A scientist. No like me, yerking and snatching, smoking like a chimney. My pal Bobby George, he says I smoke in my sleep. He should know, we've shared enough hotel rooms.

Old Bobby Dazzler, strutting around in all his gold and sequins. Ha! There's no danger of me wearing anything like that. Been a good pal to me though Bob, gets me to the gigs on time, most of the time. Was him that got me believing in myself. I ken now what I can do. I don't doubt my own ability. And I've got Bobby to thank for that.

Even still I think I play better with a glass on the table and a fag in my feed hand. Thing is, when you've been as short of the readies as I have, you're no going to say no to a free drink are you? But ken something not everybody kens about me Spike? I never touch the drink in the house. See when it's just me and Malv and the kids – never touch a drop. Quite happy with a cup of tea, happier if you must know. But, if I'm in the house, I'm no earning.

Another car goes by. JOCKY sticks his thumb out. The car doesn't stop.

Ach away and get stuffed then!

He kicks the suitcase.

Got another one like this. They come as a pair. Keep my winnings in it back at the house. Never seems to have as much in it as I think it's gonna have. Folk always asking for a loan of this and a loan of that.

He shrugs and looks down the road. He gets up and paces about looking for a car.

Hey Spike I just minded of something. Nearly had another suitcase. A braw one. No a cheap one like this. Leather and all the rest of it. Won it at the News of the World Tournament at Wembley – you heard of it? Course you havenae. You're a bloody pot plant. I beat awbody. Should have beat Stefan Lord to go into the final but I dae ken – I didnae. Ken what that Swedish laddie won? Three thousand pounds! And a holiday! Ken what I won? Aye you guessed it Spikey boy. A ruddy suitcase. Sold it on the train and spent the money in the buffet car. Came home with hee haw. All the way to London and back for a couple of bacon rolls eh?

I don't know, suitcases seem to follow me around. I remember the wee cases oor Tommy and I had when we were sent to St Margaret's. But that was –

He shakes his head as if to get rid of a thought and sits back down on the rock.

Havnae been on my own like this for a long time. Maybe ever.
There's no even that fella fae the Dole Office following me around.
Thought I'd never get rid of the nosy bastard, him wi' his beady eye
and his wee notebook. Must ha shaken him off at last.

SCENE 6 – DOLE OFFICER

JOCKY: *(As DOLE OFFICER, officious, formal Fife accent.)*

Yes I have the report sir. These are my findings in respect of John Thomas Wilson, case number 478129.

It is true I have been keeping my eye on Mr Wilson, an intermittent recipient of unemployment benefits. He came to the attention of the Department of Social Security when it became apparent he was playing darts – for money! It has since been my habit to follow Wilson – much in the style of a Philip Marlowe – to darts competitions in places such as Leven and Falkirk and even venturing on one occasion as far as Brechin. Mr Wilson's winnings were, initially, insufficient to trouble this department.

However, on Friday afternoon of last week, I was sitting in my living room watching television – I had a slight chill and Jean thought it best if I stayed indoors – when I tuned my television set to the commercial channel – which I don't usually watch but there was a costume drama on the BBC and I can't abide those – when I spotted a very familiar face. Far from seeking remunerative employment, John Thomas Wilson was competing in a darts tournament, and winning a substantial cash prize!

Mr Wilson's record of employment to date has been 'patchy'. He has previously spent brief spells as a soldier, a commis chef – apparently mastering an excellent rhubarb tart – and a 'howker' of coal. In tournament programmes he is described as 'one of the unemployed'.

Now as one of the most popular and in demand players in the country, Mr Wilson is receiving regular monies in payment for appearances in exhibitions, the true bread and butter of the darts player. In short Mr Wilson is a professional sportsman. That's right, Mr Wilson is a professional man.

And therefore is no longer one of the unemployed…for now.

JOCKY: Wanker.

SCENE 7 – THE CHEQUE

Should have seen their faces when I walked in to the Lister that night, just back from Ayrshire and with my first winner's cheque held high. They were all so chuffed it was great to see. Never knew I had so many friends.

JOCKY: *(As RAB, clutching a pint, swaying on his feet.)* What's that you're waving about there Jock? Got your giro through?

He snorts with laughter but stops when someone taps him on the arm and says something. He looks back towards JOCKY.

Eh? You're kidding! He won it?

The other person says something else.

Eh?! *How* much? Fucking hell! Hey Jocky! Well done mate! Great win. Fair proud of you pal.

To the man beside him.

Aye thought he'd make it like. Telt him that often enough. Jocky you'll do great things in the darts my son, mark my words. I always said that.

Calling across the crowded bar to JOCKY.

Aye a lager top please Jocky, that's very kind of you pal.

To the man beside him.

Known Jocky since he was wee – well wee'er than that onyways. Bet that's the most money he's seen in his puff and that's for fucking sure. Who'd a bloody thought it?

SCENE 8 – FOURTEEN FEET OF JOY

JOCKY rummages around in the case and brings out a toothbrush. He looks at it in disgust.

JOCKY: Well that's no mine!

He throws it away over his shoulder. He puts his hand in again and pulls out the water bottle. He looks at it for a moment. He breathes in and makes a stoic face as if about to drink poison.

If you ask me this stuff's better for fishing in than drinking.

He takes a swig

That's what I want like. My own wee boat. Fourteen feet of pure joy. It's no how big or how posh the boat is, that's no what it's about at all. It's that it's yours, your own, and when you're out on it, you're free. Aye, me in my woolly hat and a jersey, fishing, halfway to Norway. Couple of pieces on jam. Braw.

My dad was at sea – maybe it's something I take off him.

He gets up and walks about. He's humming 'Don't Laugh at Me Because I'm a Fool…'

Jeez I'm sweating. Feeling a bit light-headed too like. Is there no a bus stop about here? How do people get their messages?

And you know what else I'll have one day. My own pub. I think I know what makes a good boozer. Should do, I've been in one or two.

The sounds of a pub can be heard, clinking glasses, murmuring voices and juke box music.

It'll be called – wait for it – 'Jocky's Bar'. In Kirkcaldy. Not flash, just single storey. The food will be good, cooked by Malvina of course. That's my wife. And there'll be an exhibition hall with all my trophies. If I dinnae give them all away to folk. I'll have a PhD in tact by then and I'll be the perfect host.

At the end of the day I'm a simple boy and I dinnae want much.

Pause.

Never did really. Suppose that comes from being brought up in a children's home? I mean it wasnae what you'd have asked for. No always the easiest thing at school, being one of the 'home' kids eh? I was good at the school like, no brilliant, but alright. Played football. I had trials for Fife. And I was in the cricket team,

Mimes hitting an elegant shot.

I'll have you know.

Pause.

Was at St Margaret's House Orphanage 'til I was eighteen. I thought it was perfectly pleasant. I did. They looked after me well enough and I'm grateful for that. I wasnae sent there for being a being a bad boy Spike you understand. Was just that my mum and dad, they split up. But it was fine. It was. You'll get a different story from my wee brother Tommy like. He curses the place. I never understood why.

Pause. JOCKY looks at his watch and shakes his head.

SCENE 9 – TOM

JOCKY: Peter Purves. Mind o' that bugger wi' the sticky back plastic
and all the rest of it? Was interviewed by him recently. 'Bout my life.
For the BBC. Probably the last time I spent as long thinking about
the past. Don't do it often. No like our Tom. He spends a lot of time
thinking about when we were kids and that. And his version's no
barrel of laughs.

JOCKY: *(As TOM, rougher, more emotional version of JOCKY's voice.)* Does
everything have to be a laugh Jocky? Do you have to be entertaining
awbody all the time?

JOCKY: I says, What do you mean? That's one of the things I enjoy most
about the darts. Entertaining folk, making them laugh.

Pause.

Tom he says to me, 'Will you mention me Jock, in your interview?

And I'm like what, do you think they want to hear about your thievin'
and your fightin'? I don't think so.

And he's still asking the questions, going like, you gonna talk about
St Margaret's? I just told him I said, I'll mention it. Will say it was
pleasant.

TOM: *Pleasant?* Fuck's sake Jocky. What sort of fucking word is that?
How can it be pleasant being brought up in an orphanage when your
mother and father and your brothers and sisters are living, thegither,
just along the road. How can that be pleasant?

Things were worse than you remember them John. Why'd they send
you and me away? Was it because we were one big happy family? The
fucking Waltons of Kirkcaldy?

Same old Jocky, never ask questions never complain. Aye easy going.
Aye happy as Larry as long as you were warm and fed.

Mind o' when you started in the darts and you had nothing, and
Jocky you didnae always look so great. Your hair, it needed brushing
and your clothes were a state. Mind o that? Your manager, what was

it he said? 'Jocky doesn't need a manager, he needs a mother!'

But there was aye somebody, somebody like Mrs Blyth, would pay your bus fare to the matches. Aye somebody who'd buy you a drink or put up your entry money. Why'd they do that Jock?

JOCKY: Maybe they thought I could be a great player. Better than they could be. Maybe they knew I had the hunger. The steel. Maybe. Maybe they just liked me. And wanted to help me.

Pause. To the cactus:

She did come and visit us, my mother. We walked on the beach at Elie. She was aye saying she didn't want to miss the last bus. There again, she did have eight other kids to look after right enough. Maybe she didn't like seeing us there.

SCENE 10 – CRAFTY COCKNEY

JOCKY nervously paces about humming. He looks at his watch. He's becoming more anxious, a bit hysterical.

JOCKY: Get me out of this place! Sand and dust and more bloody sand. This isnae the Lang Toun that's for sure, just a lang bloody road!

He suddenly ducks, at the sound of huge beating wings. He covers his face with his arms, shielding it from something above.

Jesus, what a size of a bird! S'like a bloody flying turkey.

He holds his hand over his heart.

Maybe be needing they extra underpants after all.

He cranes his neck and looks up at the circling bird.

It's a vulture, a fucking vulture! Can you believe it?! Obviously doesnae fancy the wee Fifer's chances out here in the sun.

He picks up a stone and hurls it at the bird.

Get to – beat it! Consider that a warning shot. If you'd been seven and a half feet away you'd be deid.

It's away. Thank god. What a bloody fright to get.

I'm no' usually ever feart of things. You've got to have bottle in my game. Your opponents, and the crowd, can give you pelters like but I just give it right back. Although I'll be honest, now and again the verbals can get to me. I reckon there's some that knows that and try to use it against me.

Played a match, against one of the greats it was, that left me in tears with the tension and the bitterness. And I don't care who knows it. Clicking my darts? I was doing no such thing. And he wasnae happy about my smoking neither. Bastard knew I had a suspension hanging over me and was trying to get me going.

Darts, when you get right to the heart of it –

He points to his head.

The competition's up here. And it's not for everyone to put themselves through that. In front of awbody as well.

Sometimes when you're up there on the oche, on your own, with the punters at your back all expecting you to play like a champion, to hit everything, when you're on song it's magic. You feel like you could fly. But when you're aim's off, you cannae concentrate, you're tired. The crowd they soon let you know they're no impressed. They expect tons and ton pluses all the time from a pro and they're merciless if you don't come up with the goods. It's back to the practice, the hours and hours you have to put in so you can play sixteen opponents over three hours, score six to eight 180s and hit your doubles every time.

Talent and practice are no enough though. You have to be a showman. The public expect a performance.

He does jazz hands.

A few jokes. Half an hour on the mike at the end. So they want you laughing but at the same time taking the darts deadly seriously. Enjoying a drink but still being able to throw straight. It's a knife edge.
Aye it's kill or be killed up on that oche. Gotta keep your game down to the 15 dart level to compete at the top. But it's no personal in our game, not at all.

Although there's one opponent I've played a few times who I really want to beat. Eric. Bristow. They dinnae like it down south when this wee Scots bulldog beats their man but that just makes me play better, faster, more accurate. Bristow, he comes in to the players' lounge and starts giving it a' this –

JOCKY jumps up onto the rock to imitate the much taller BRISTOW.

(Cockney accent.) Why did you lot even bother turning up tonight eh? There's only gonna be one winner.

JOCKY jumps down and looks up as if to BRISTOW.

Aye we'll see about that ya big lank.

To the cactus.

See I'm one of the few to stand up to him.

Jumps on rock.

Go on Jocky have another drink, you've time for another one – or six – before the match.

Jumps down.

Aye you'll no get me that way.

Jumps up.

No? I have before.

Jumps down.

I ken what's going on. You think everyone wants to see the big English favourite, the Crafty Cockney, beat the wee Scotsman. But they dinnae, they cannae stand you!

Jumps up.

Water off a duck's back mate! Don't care if they love me or hate me, I'm here to win. Get out of the way shortie. I hope you've got a return ticket to Scotchland.

Jumps down, puffed out. Turns to the cactus.

It's hard work being that tall! Bristow, the prince of patter they call him. Prince of pish more like. Brilliant player mind, I'll gie him that. Hey I must have that sunstroke if I'm being nice about Bristow. No, no, I'd no have a problem shaking the bastard's hand. In fact, I like to applaud the other fella's play. That's just good darts.

Pause.

The officials though, that's a different story. It's harder to take a loss when you realise it's the officials you've been playing against.

SCENE 11 – HONOLULU

As he says this, JOCKY goes into the throwing position. Suddenly he looks over his shoulder, paranoid.

JOCKY: *(As OFFICIAL, Northern English accent.)* You really need to calm yourself down Mr Wilson or you will forfeit this match.

JOCKY: *(Heated.)* Eh? There's six thousand quid riding on this. Hard enough to concentrate without some bugger trying to put me off my stride. And that wifey in the blue jacket. She's up to something. She's meant to be counting score fair and square, no favourites. But the way she's saying it, the way she's behaving, she definitely wants that other fella to win. I'll be having a word with her later. That's no on like. This is all tricky enough wi' out folk taking sides.

OFFICIAL: I'm going to have to ask you to step back. Language like that will not be tolerated!

JOCKY: And this guy, can he no bloody count? Was he off the day they were teaching arithmetic at the school? There's no way that finish is right. I'm counting myself and I'm never wrong. He's just a stupit bloody–

OFFICIAL: Enough! I don't take kindly to you accusing our trained officials of miscounting. It's gonna be a ban for you Wilson!

JOCKY: Banned??!!

A few bars of Hawaiian music is heard.

(As if reading from a postcard, pretending to play a small guitar and swaying his hips.)
Dear all. Sorry to be missing the British Professional Darts Championship. Being banned is not so bad after all. Enjoying playing here in Honolulu. Ten thousand pound first prize up for grabs! Wish you were here. All the best, Jocky.

Life eh? Aye throwing you off course. Never thought I'd be stuck out here in the bloody High Chaparral with a match to get to. S'no funny any more. Been out here for hours!

But it's how you react, whether you can think on your feet. Like the finishes in a game. Soon as you miss, you have to come up with another way to get there, to win. There's a hell of a lot of mathematical possibilities to deal with, especially under pressure.

JOCKY: *(As COMMENTATOR.)* Jocky you require 119!

JOCKY: That's treble 20, treble 19 and double 1. But what if I miss that treble 19 and hit a single instead? You cannae let your mind dwell on the mistake. I still need 40 so double top to finish. If you've practised hard enough you learn the finishes. You ken thousands of them.

COMMENTATOR: Jocky you require 131!

JOCKY: That's treble 20, treble 17 and a double 10. Got to finish on a double.

COMMENTATOR: Jocky you require 157!

JOCKY: Treble 20, a treble 19 and then double top.

Pause.

They doubles can get you though. You can play brilliant darts all night and still lose on the double. If I miss a double that would have won a crucial game, I'll throw it for an hour the next day. That's how your mind builds up a store of confidence in shots.

COMMENTATOR: Jocky you require 101!

JOCKY: Exhibition stuff. Bull, single one and a bull again for a cheeky 101!

He lies down, with his head resting on a rock at the foot of the cactus. He starts to nod off.

When you think about it that's a strange thing about the darts. You start with a big score and aim to end up with nothing.

SCENE 12 – COALTOWN OF BALGONIE

The exhausted and dehydrated JOCKY is confused to hear a phone ring. He picks up the bottle of water and holds it to his ear.

JOCKY: Hello?

DRIVER: *(V.O., Geordie accent.)* John! Your favourite driver here! Glad you're up. Thought I might have to come and shake you out of your pit!

JOCKY: *(Uncertainly.)* Aye I'm up. I'm ready.

DRIVER: Sound more enthusiastic John. I heard the pay's magic and who wouldn't fancy a trip to wonderful, wonderful Copenhagen?

JOCKY: There's no an exhibition in wonderful, wonderful Coaltown of Balgonie is there?

DRIVER: Where the fuck's that then?

JOCKY: It's just along the road fae the house. Nice wee place –

DRIVER: *(Cutting across him.)* Sorry you're breaking up a bit there John. Listen, sponsor's a beer company so you'll have to get a few pints down your neck to keep 'em sweet.

JOCKY: Sounds good. Danish beer's no bad like.

DRIVER: Too right! So get your wee case packed up again and I'll be there in an hour or so.

JOCKY: *(With forced enthusiasm.)* Great. I'm ready. Ready for Denmark and your Hans Christian Anderson.

DRIVER: I think it's Lazarenko you're playing isn't it? Anyway get you're arse in gear John!

JOCKY: Oh aye I'll be there.

JOCKY puts the bottle down and lies back. As he is drifting off,

So it's Copenhagen I'm going to, no Vegas. It's aye somewhere, somewhere that's not Fife.

The phone immediately rings again. The voice of the DRIVER shouting 'wake up' combines with the shriek of the returning vulture to wake JOCKY.

SCENE 13 – COYOTE

The light is dimming. Another car engine can be heard, getting closer. JOCKY tries to flag it down but the car sweeps on by. JOCKY crouches over, hands on knees.

JOCKY: Nawwwww! Starting to lose it here. I just want tae go HOME!!!!

He drinks the last of the water.

My lips are all cracked to blazes and I'm gaspin' on a cup of tea. See this is when you just want to be in your armchair, *Grandstand* on the telly, the kids all doing their thing, my dad seeing to his roses out the front of the bungalow, Malvina…

(He whispers.) Malvina!

Ken this Spike? Malvina, she picked totties so I could practise when I started. What a woman. Fae Argentina ye ken. We've had some stick for that which is a wee shame.

Know what I was doing when I met her? Howking coal. Black I was, head to toe. But Malv, even though I was covered in shite, she could still see I was braw like.

Like I said, St Margaret's, it wasnae a problem but it's no like your own home is it? No like what I've got with Malv and the wee ones. Married at eighteen we were. Once you've got that, you dinnae want to leave.

He stands, head lowered. Suddenly a coyote howls in the near distance. JOCKY jumps.

WHAT THE FUCK WAS THAT?!

JOCKY is terrified and distressed. He paces, his hand over his eyes. He stops suddenly.

Right, that's it. Enough. I've had it. I cannae do this any more. I love the darts, I do, but I'm sick to the stomach of the travelling and the pressure and the being away from home, always thinking my luck's just about to leave me, having to make the most of it when I can. People think it's a fine and dandy life but I'm up and down that motorway seven days a week. Sleeping in the car to save a bit of cash, living off hotdogs and fizzy juice. It cannae be doing me any good.

I'm miles from home, there's vultures and fucking werewolves out there and I've not got a brass farthing on me.

Face it Jock, the only thing you're any good at is hitting a dartboard from seven and a half feet away. And even then it's no pretty. You're nothin' but an embarrassment.

SCENE 14 – MAGIC BEANS

JOCKY rattles through a sequence of voices from his past.

> *(RAB.)* Jocky Wilson? Nothing but an embarrassment…he'll never
> be world champion…*(BRISTOW)*…could be a Scottish sporting
> great…there'll be a statue of him in Kirkcaldy one day…*(OFFICIAL.)*
> lets the drink get the better of him…nasty when he's had a few…
> *(TOM.)* You were my hero Jock…why'd they send me and you away?
> *(HUSTLER.)*…best in the world? Ha! Better hit the road Jacky…
> *(DOLE OFFICER.)* playing darts for money…will always be one of
> the unemployed…*(RAB.)* may as well gie up afore you start Jock …
> an embarrassment…world champion…my hero…embarrassment…
> world champion…my hero…world champion…champion.'

*JOCKY kicks the suitcase, spilling its few contents, including his three darts. He
picks them up, rolls them in his fingers and holds one up high as if about to throw.
He looks at it intently.*

JOCKY: What the fuck am I thinking about? Why should I bloody give
up? I've got the talent. I know I have. Nobody's as hungry as I am.
There's folk depending on me and Christ the nerves, the drink, a bit
of travelling, some tough opponents – they're no the hardest things
I've had to deal with in my time.

See when you're good at something, really good, better than everyone
else? It's like the magic fucking beans eh, something you can trade for
a new life.

Come on, Jocky come on. You shouldnae ha let yourself get so…so…
lost!

Thing is, my start in life, it wasnae the best but it wasnae the worst either.
I've made my life about the darts and the darts has made me a better
person. I've practised and I've played and I've taken them all on and I've
got to the point where, and I'm not boasting here like, I'm one of the best
darts players in the world. In the world! That's something eh? Is that no
enough?!

And I can be the world champion. I know I can. Keep my aim steady and it'll be Jocky Wilson Champion of the World and me and my family we'll have some party I'll tell you.

Truth is, so far, I've hit everything I want to hit.

He stabs the three darts into the cactus, punctuating his words.

And at the end of the day, the only person responsible for everything that's happened to me, for everything that's gonna happen to me, is *(He thumps his chest.)*
Me!

The coyote howls again. This time JOCKY is less fearful. He jumps up on the rock and tries to look out into the night.

I hear you, you stupid yankee mutt. Think I'm feart of you? Seen scarier dugs in Beveridge Park!

SCENE 15 – GAME ON

It's getting darker and JOCKY's hopes of getting to the match are fading.

He looks at his watch.

But I'm still not gonna make it. Thought I was gonna…

He sighs.

My dad's old watch. Willie. He enjoys my success. Never had much of his own.

A faint strain of music can be heard. The song is Norman Wisdom's 'Don't Laugh at Me Because I'm a Fool'. JOCKY lifts his head.

Hey Spike – do you hear that?

He hums along.

That's ma dad's tune.

He hums along a bit more.

His party piece. We sing it thegither when there's a sing song in the pub.

He joins in with the song, singing it with unexpected sweetness. As he sways to the music, he interrupts himself to comment to the cactus:

You dancing Spike?

He reaches out to the cactus but leaps away as he jags his finger. He resumes singing but as he reaches the line 'I see…' he spots something in the distance.

I see – A CAR I SEE A CAR!

A faint engine sound can be heard getting louder. JOCKY frantically tries to wave it down.

Hey!

Hey there!

Mister!

The car engine gets louder and then stops.

Ya beauty!

JOCKY: Hey pal you going to Vegas aye? Las Vegas? You know it?

Aye? Magic!

He pumps the air with his fist and turns to go back for his case. He then turns again to the driver of the car.

Hey mate, you are real aren't you? You're no' a bloody collage? Been having a funny old time of it here the day.

That's good then. Just wanted to check.

He puts the pants back in the suitcase and closes it up. He pauses, looking around the desert expanse. He addresses the cactus for the last time.

JOCKY: That's me away then Spike. Got myself a lift. Can you believe it? I tell you, seems you're as lucky as you're unlucky in this life and that's the truth of it.

JOCKY looks at his watch.

Looks like I am gonna bloody make it after all. Just. Tell you, for a second there I thought I was going doolally. Anyway, nice to meet you.

As he is about to leave the stage, he runs back and pulls the darts out of the cactus.

No gonna be winning anything without these – GAME ON!

He exits. We hear more radio static and bright light surrounds the stage –

COMMENTARY: *(V.O., loud)* And Jocky wins! The victor takes the plaudits. Thanks the officials. And yes there are tears. There will be singing, highland flinging all over Scotland tonight. Jocky Wilson is the World Professional Darts Champion of 1982!

The End.

DO NOT PRESS THIS BUTTON

Alan Bissett

Alan Bissett is a playwright, novelist and performer who grew up in Falkirk and now lives in Renfrewshire with his partner and two children. His most well-known plays are *The Moira Monologues*, *The Ching Room*, *Turbo Folk* and *The Pure, the Dead and the Brilliant*.

Do Not Press This Button was first performed
at Òran Mór as part of A Play, A Pie and A Pint
on Monday 11 November, 2019.

Directed by Kirstin McLean

Cast: Gemma McElhinney, David Rankine and
Cameron Fulton

Empty train carriage in the middle of the day. BEN and MARIA get on, choose their seats, stow their luggage, get themselves sorted for the journey, all to the sound of the mighty opening build-up to 'Money for Nothing' by Dire Straits, which MARIA is listening to on her earphones.

She sits at one table, BEN sits at another. BEN is swiping at his phone and MARIA is reading her book. BEN keeps looking at MARIA, as though summoning the courage to talk to her.

BEN: Good book?

MARIA takes her buds out of her ears. The Dire Straits song cuts out.

MARIA: Sorry?

BEN: The book you're reading. Is it any good?

MARIA: Em. Yes. Yes it is.

She puts her earbuds back in, goes back to reading. BEN works up to another question.

BEN: What is it?

MARIA: Huh?

She takes her earbuds out.

BEN: What book is it?

MARIA: The Holy Bible.

BEN: Oh. Well, em, I won't interrupt you if you're having a spiritual mom—

She shows him her book.

BEN: Ian Rankin. Ha ha okay. That's a relief.

MARIA: Why's it a relief?

BEN: I was worried for a second you were a Bible-basher.

She takes a crucifix out from below her neckline and shows it to him.

MARIA: I am.

BEN: Ah.

MARIA: Maybe in future try not to judge people, okay?

She goes to put her earphones back in. BEN gives an ironic laugh and she stops.

MARIA: What's funny?

BEN: 'Don't judge people.' You *might* wanna tell that to the big guy upstairs…

MARIA: Excuse me, is there a reason why you're being so rude?

BEN: Oh dear. Look, uh, this isn't how I imagined it going at all.

MARIA: Imagined what going?

BEN: Okay, I'll be honest. I've noticed you on this journey loads of times, same one as me, going up and down the country. But apart from the odd tourist, sometimes we're the only people in the carriage. You've seen me before, right?

MARIA: I recognise your face.

BEN: But we've never spoken to each other.

MARIA: Why do we need to speak to each other?

BEN: Well, we don't *need* to. But we see each other all the time, so why not? Everyone sits on trains staring into their phones or listening to music, ignoring the people we share the journey with. Do you not look at folk and wonder who they are, or what their lives are like?

MARIA: I mind my own business.

BEN: Okay, point taken. But… I think we're just missing out on a human experience. It's happening all around us, all the time. But we don't care.

He catches himself.

BEN: Look. I'm sorry, I probably sound like a total weirdo now. I don't mean to bother you. Go back to your book, it's fine.

He lifts his phone.

MARIA: No, you've got my attention.

BEN: Have I?

MARIA: Put your phone down.

He does.

MARIA: Let's find out about each other.

BEN: I mean, only if that's alright with y–

MARIA: When did you lose your virginity?

BEN: Uh sorry, what?

MARIA: Your virginity. What age did you lose it?

BEN: That's kind of a personal question.

She starts reading her book again. After a while...

BEN: Twenty-one.

A handsome man, TERRY, walks through the carriage.

MARIA: You lost your virginity when you were *twenty-one?*

BEN: Shh!

TERRY stops by them.

BEN: Don't listen to her, she's just having a laugh. You didn't hear that, did you?

TERRY shrugs.

TERRY: Is there usually a guy with a wee trolley on this train?

MARIA: Yes. But he's been through already.

TERRY: Aw, did I miss him?

BEN: Did he not come past you?

TERRY: Was sleepin. Up late last night.

He lets that hang there.

BEN: Um, partying?

TERRY: Let's go with that word for it, aye.

He winks at BEN. BEN catches on.

BEN: Ah. Well, alright for some eh?

TERRY: Exactly, mate!

He slaps BEN's arm, then turns to MARIA.

TERRY: I don't mean to be crude. Sorry, love.

MARIA: It's fine, em, *sweetheart*.

TERRY: Right, time for a beer.

MARIA looks at her watch.

TERRY: What? It's past twelve, likes.

MARIA: Mate, I don't care. Fire on.

TERRY: Yese wanting me tay get yese wan?

MARIA shakes her head.

BEN: No, thank you.

He gives them the thumbs up, then moves down the carriage and out. BEN watches him go.

MARIA: Thank god. I thought he was going to sit down.

BEN: That was inappropriate.

MARIA: You're telling me. Four minutes past twelve and he's getting torn in?

BEN: No, I mean asking when I lost my virginity.

MARIA: It was you who wanted us to 'find out' about each other.

She goes back to her book.

BEN: So do I get to…?

MARIA: Do you get to what?

BEN: Do I get to ask you a question?

MARIA: No.

BEN: C'mon I answered yours.

MARIA: Fair enough. ONE. You can ask one.

BEN: Okay, what –

MARIA: NOT what age I lost my virginity.

BEN: Sure. Um. What's your favourite film?

MARIA: *Gone With The Wind*. It's timeless.

BEN: Even with all the stuff about, um, slavery and that? You think?

MARIA: I do. That okay with you?

BEN: Frankly, my dear, I don't give a damn.

She acknowledges the joke.

BEN: Your turn.

MARIA: Oh, are we still going?

BEN: If you want to. But let's just agree that each of us has one veto, for a question they don't like.

MARIA: Fair enough. If I get bored or you start to annoy me, I can go back to my book and you'll go back to your phone. Agreed?

BEN: Agreed.

He moves over to her table and sits across from her. She's a wee bit surprised, but okay.

MARIA: So, uh…what do your parents do?

BEN: Mum's a primary school teacher. Dad was in the army, but he's retired now. Uh, what's your favourite city in the world?

MARIA: Vienna.

BEN makes a face.

MARIA: What's wrong with Vienna?

BEN: It means nothing to me.

MARIA: Oh you're full of the patter you, eh? Um…do you have any pets?

BEN: A tarantula.

MARIA: A tarantula? You're not a weird spider guy, are you? Like, you invite folk back and get the tarantula out?

BEN: Of course I do. There's no point in having a tarantula if you're not going to show it off. They're lovely, gentle creatures. We project all these fears onto them, make them into monsters. They've no reason to bite you.

MARIA: They're creepy.

BEN: You're just stereotyping. Arachnophobia's a real problem for the spider community. Cos of bigots like you.

MARIA: Guilty.

BEN: Okay, if you were left alone in a room with a button below a sign that said Do Not Press This Button…would you press it?

MARIA: *Immediately.*

BEN: Yeah?

MARIA: Well, this whole conversation is a button marked Do Not Press.

BEN: And yet.

MARIA: I pressed it.

BEN: You pressed it.

MARIA: Whose turn is it?

BEN: Yours.

MARIA: Favourite colour?

BEN: Purple. I used to be a Goth. Favourite book?

MARIA: *Lord of the Rings.*

BEN: Ugh. *Lord of the Rings* is just….porridge for the brain.

MARIA: *Lord of the Rings* is genius so you shut your goddamn whore mouth.

BEN is taken aback, before he realises she's playing. She points finger-guns.

MARIA: Favourite vegetable?

BEN: Mushrooms. Little button ones. Favourite superhero?

MARIA: Catwoman.

BEN: Catwoman's a villain.

MARIA: Well, that depends on your point of view. *(Purrs.)*

BEN: Good answer.

MARIA: *Miaow.* Favourite race?

BEN: Oh, the Grand National. I put a flutter on it every year. Just a habit.

MARIA: Haha, no. I mean favourite *race.*

BEN: Race? Like, what do you mean 'race'?

MARIA: Like, race. RACE.

She moves her hand around in front of her face.

BEN: Oh. You mean, like, somebody's race? Like their…*racial* race?

MARIA: Yeah.

BEN: Nobody's ever asked me that before.

MARIA: That's why it's a good question.

BEN: Can I use my veto on that one?

MARIA: You can. But that's interesting, isn't it?

BEN: Why's that interesting?

MARIA: Just that of all the questions I've asked *that's* the one you're using a veto on. The one about race.

BEN: Well, race is kinda personal.

MARIA: More personal than asking when you lost your virginity? You answered that one.

BEN: Yes. But, uh…

MARIA: And how can your race be 'personal'? It's right there on your face. Everyone can see it.

BEN: I know, but. What's your…your motive?

MARIA: My 'motive' is to find out what your favourite race is. We've said favourite films, books, cities. What's the harm in saying your favourite race?

BEN: I don't really have a favourite.

MARIA: Oh, what? You like all races equally?

BEN: Yes. All equal. All the same.

MARIA: So you like the pygmy tribe of Southern Borneo just the same as you like…the Irish?

BEN: Are the Irish a race?

MARIA: Well, you tell me. Then tell me whether or not they're your favourite.

BEN: Sorry, I used my veto.

MARIA: Okay then. Your question.

BEN: Um… What's your, uh, favourite album?

MARIA: Of any artist? Of all time? *Brothers in Arms* by Dire Straits.

BEN: That's a good album.

MARIA: It *is* a good album. It's a *bloody* good album.

BEN: Mine is probably *Dusty in Memphis*, or maybe *Grace* by Jeff Buckl–

MARIA: I didn't ask.

BEN: What?

MARIA: I didn't ask what your favourite album is. That's not my next question.

BEN: What's your next question?

MARIA: Do you prefer the pygmy tribes of Southern Borneo to the Irish?

BEN: Ah. Like I said. Veto.

MARIA: You've used your veto.

BEN: It's the same question though.

MARIA: It isn't. The last question was 'What's your favourite race?' This question is 'Do you prefer the pygmy tribes of Southern Borneo to the Irish?'

BEN: Are you Irish?

MARIA: First of all, it's not your turn to ask a question. Second, do I sound Irish?

BEN: No.

MARIA: No. So what's your favourite between the pygmy tribes of Souther—

BEN: Okay, okay I heard you!

MARIA: I'm not sure you did, cos you've not answered.

BEN: I suppose, given… I've been to Ireland…and I've never been to Borneo, let alone Southern Borneo, let alone met a pygmy there… I suppose I'd say…the Irish.

MARIA: There you go, that wasn't too hard, was it? So it *is* possible to prefer a race.

BEN: I never said the Irish were my *favourite*.

MARIA: No, but you demonstrated that even someone who claims he likes all races equally *can*, in fact, like one more than the other, based on familiarity. So the race you're most familiar with is probably your favourite.

BEN: Will that be the next question? Which race am I most familiar with?

MARIA: No. It *was* going to be, 'What's your favourite track on *Brothers in Arms* by Dire Straits?' but actually your question's better. So which race are you most familiar with?

BEN: I think it's my turn.

She thinks back.

MARIA: You asked what my favourite album was… I asked the thing about the pygmies and the Irish… No, you're right. It is your question.

BEN: Right, um. What's your favourite track on *Brothers in Arms* by Dire Straits?

MARIA: That is hard to answer. Cos there are so many good songs on it. I mean, you've got 'Money For Nothing', 'Walk of Life', 'Brothers in Arms'…

BEN: Great singles.

MARIA: Probably 'The Man's Too Strong'.

BEN: Oh yeah, that's a cracker.

They sing the first few lines of the chorus, culminating with–

MARIA & BEN: 'The man's too big. The man's too STRONG.'

BEN: Ha ha ha.

MARIA: DOOOWW! DOOOOW Ch-ch!

MARIA & BEN: DOOOWW! DOOOOW! Ch-ch!

BEN: Hahaha. It's like they're in the room.

MARIA: I wish Dire Straits would go back on tour. I'd see them every night. Anyway. My question.

BEN: Go on.

MARIA: Which race are you most familiar with?

BEN: Oh for godsakes!

MARIA: What's the matter now?

BEN: Why are all your questions about race?

MARIA: They're not all about race. I asked about your mum's job, I asked if you have any pets...

BEN: Veto. Veto.

MARIA: You've used your veto.

BEN: Oh I don't know then! Asians!

MARIA: Asians?

BEN: Asians.

MARIA: The race you're most familiar with is Asians?

BEN: Asians, yeah. The man who runs my corner shop is Asian and I'm in there every day to buy a paper and I chat away to him and his family. They're nice people.

MARIA: Right. So are this guy and his family, like, the only people you know?

BEN: What?

MARIA: You have friends and family of your own?

BEN: Of course I do. What are you on about?

MARIA: Would you say you're more familiar with this Asian guy and his family than you are with your own family?

BEN: Obviously not!

MARIA: So clearly Asians aren't the race you're most familiar with.

BEN: What? No. Wait. What?

MARIA: I'll spell it out for you. Are most of your friends and family white?

BEN: Yes.

MARIA: Well there you are.

BEN: There I am what?

MARIA: You're more familiar with white people than you are with Asian people.

BEN: Well, yes. So?

MARIA: SO. Why don't you just say your favourite race is white people?

BEN: Because white people are NOT my favourite race.

MARIA: They're not? What percentage of your friends, family, acquaintances would you say are listed as 'Caucasian' on a census?

BEN: I dunno!

MARIA: Roughly.

BEN: Roughly? I mean. How do I even…? Jeez. About…ninety percent?

MARIA: Ninety percent?

BEN: Yeah. Yeah, about ninety percent.

MARIA: If someone listened to Dire Straits ninety percent of the time, would you say that was their favourite band?

She raises her hands.

MARIA: At least I'm owning it.

BEN: I've nothing to 'own'!

MARIA: Oh don't you? You have a friendship group comprised of ninety percent one race and you find it impossible to say that's your favourite? Look at this picture. What does it tell you?

BEN: I suppose. *Technically*. That does make white people my 'favourite' race. *Technically*.

MARIA: No 'technically' about it. Look, you found it easier to say that you liked Irish and Asian people than you did to say you liked your own race. Your own people. Even though the Irish and the Muslims–

BEN: I didn't say the people who run my corner shop were Muslims! Although they do observe Ramadan. Carry on.

MARIA: Even though the Irish and the Muslims have literally bombed mainland Britain, murdered innocent British civilians, just going about their daily business, shopping, or picking somebody up from town, or heading for a pint with their mates. Here one second, the next dead. Is it that? Is it that what made you choose them before us?

BEN: No, no, you're twisting my wor –

MARIA: I mean, the pygmies of Southern Borneo have never done any harm to you, but they weren't even in the running!

BEN: What 'running'? This is absurd!

MARIA: Come on. Be honest. Would you feel relaxed sitting on a train next to a guy with dark skin and the full beard, grabbing onto his rucksack for dear life, the Koran open in front of him, muttering away in Arabic? You telling me you wouldn't even feel a flicker of nervousness?

BEN: Possibly a…flicker.

MARIA: But you felt relaxed enough around *me* to ask what book I was reading? You still kept speaking to me, even after I showed you a religious symbol. But it's fine, cos I'm white. Does that not tell you something about what your favourite race actually is?

BEN: Okay. Right. It's my question now.

MARIA: Fire away.

BEN: Since you're so keen to ask the probing questions about the edgy issues. Y'know. So sure that I'm a racist.

MARIA: I never said you were a racist. I just said it's obvious you love white people.

BEN: Right. Right. So let's turn it around. What's *your* favourite race?

MARIA: The Inuits.

BEN: The…the Inuits?

MARIA: Aye, from the North Pole. And Northern Canada. Alaska, place likes that.

BEN: Inuits. Not…not white people?

MARIA: Oh no, white people are terrible. White people are always about one riot away from fascism. White people make me sick.

BEN: Right. That's…not what I thought you were going to say.

MARIA: The Inuits are much nicer than white people.

BEN: So you're telling me that ninety percent of the people you know are Inuit?

MARIA: No, I wouldn't say that.

BEN: Ah-ha!

MARIA: But I did live among them for two years. And I'll tell you this, I prefer them to white people any day of the week. I try to talk to white people as little as I can. I mean, I'm stuck in this country for now, so it's hard for me to avoid them. And every so often you'll get an interesting conversation from them. In fact, this has been one. Thanks. It was nice chatting to you.

She puts in her earbuds, goes back to her book, leaving BEN staring at her dumfounded.

BEN: No. No. Wait.

She takes out her earbuds.

MARIA: What is it?

BEN: I'm not having that.

MARIA: Not having what?

BEN: Any of it.

MARIA: Look. I'm sure you're a lovely guy. But *you* interrupted *me*. I was quite happy reading, but you saw fit to try and demand my time. I've given you my time. And I've been perfectly polite. Now I'd like to go back to my book please. That was the deal, wasn't it? That you'd let me do that?

She starts reading. BEN is flabbergasted.

BEN: No. No way. Hang on.

MARIA: What is it now?

BEN: What do you mean you hate white people?

MARIA: Was I unclear? I hate them. I. Fucking. Hate them.

BEN: But you're white.

MARIA: So?

BEN: So you hate yourself?

MARIA: No, I don't hate myself. I'm a lovely person. I can't help what colour skin I was born with.

BEN: So you hate me?

MARIA: No, I don't hate you. You seem alright. I've noticed you're not content to let me get back to my book though, so that could change.

BEN: But in the main, you hate white people?

MARIA: Yes. They disgust me. Well no, hang on, that's not fair.

BEN: Oh you *think*?

MARIA: Just the men.

BEN: Just…the men?

MARIA: White men have essentially captured the entire globe and bent it to their will, while keeping their boots pressed down on the heads of every other race on earth. White men have been responsible for more genocide, colonialism and slavery than any other race in history. White men have amassed so much of the world's wealth and resources through theft and violence it's INSANE. But, then again, white men wrote *Brothers in Arms* by Dire Straits. There you go. That's a positive to end on!

She goes back to her book. BEN is fuming.

BEN: Wait. Wait. Who first landed on the Moon?

MARIA: Neil Armstrong, obviously.

BEN: Mm-hm. And who invented penicillin?

MARIA: Alexander Fleming?

BEN: Correct. And how about the human genome? Who discovered the human genome?

MARIA: Actually, I don't know that one.

BEN: Francis Crick and James Watson!

MARIA: Well I never.

BEN: And what do they have in common?

MARIA: They're all clever?

BEN: They are indeed. And what else?

MARIA: They all pooped and burped?

BEN: Try again.

MARIA: Nope, can't think. You'll just have to tell me.

BEN: They're white men!

MARIA: Oh. So they are.

BEN: You see? You see what I'm saying?

MARIA: Hm, you're right. White men are *great*. Would you go as far as to say they're your favourite?

She goes back to her book.

BEN: How dare you.

MARIA: Excuse me?

BEN: You said it yourself. Those people bombed us.

MARIA: 'Those people'?

BEN: The Irish. The Muslims. 'Murdered innocent British civilians', I believe you said.

MARIA: That is part of the historical record, yes.

BEN: So now they're your friends?

MARIA: No no no, I said Inuits were my friends. I've never been to Ireland. And I don't really know many Asians very well, if I'm being honest with you. The Inuits though? Gorgeous people–

BEN: My father. Right. *My father* fought in the British army.

MARIA: Um. Okay.

BEN: Fought for my freedom. For your freedom. Your freedom as a woman.

MARIA: What do you mean 'as a woman'?

BEN: You know they don't even let you drive a car?

MARIA: The army?

BEN: Muslims! Saudi Arabia! Women, banned from driving cars. Not allowed to vote. Stoned to death for the 'crime' of having extra-marital sex.

MARIA: Well, I'm glad I don't live there.

BEN: Not just that. Homosexuality is illegal too. In fact, do you know how many Muslim countries will execute someone just for being gay?

MARIA: How many?

BEN: I don't know but it's a lot! They think loving another man means you should be sentenced to death. But no no no, it's the WHITE people that are the problem, eh?

MARIA: Mate. You're getting a bit worked up. Calm down.

BEN: Homosexuality was illegal in Ireland until 1993. 1993! Twenty-six years *after* it was decriminalised in the UK. Did you know that?

MARIA: I did know that, actually.

BEN: Well then!

BEN folds his arms and looks out the window, raging. MARIA regrets pushing him too far. TERRY comes back through the carriage, drinking from a bottle of beer. He puts that plus two more bottles down on the table that BEN was at before.

TERRY: You not sitting here anymore, mate?

BEN shakes his head. MARIA looks up and down the empty carriage, wondering why TERRY's chosen there of all places.

TERRY: Everything alright?

MARIA smiles sweetly at him.

MARIA: Absolutely fine, thanks for asking.

TERRY nods and points to his beers.

TERRY: I'm away for a pish. Keep an eye on them, eh?

MARIA: 'Please'?

TERRY: Please, aye, sorry.

TERRY: Dinnay drink them!

MARIA: Well dinnay leave them.

TERRY laughs and exits.

MARIA: Why's he sitting there? Carriage is empty...

BEN, in a huff, just shrugs.

MARIA: Look...

BEN: What?

MARIA: I don't hate *all* of you.

BEN: Oh, not *all* of us?

MARIA: No. Some of my best friends are white.

He raises his hand: enough.

MARIA: Let me explain. The Inuits have got this culture of...honesty, of speaking your mind. They see it as necessary for the...unity of the tribe, so that nobody's hiding their feelings and resentments don't build up. That's all I was doing. Speaking honestly.

BEN: So honest it near cut my face open.

MARIA: It's funny, see being back here? Somehow it's less honest but more…tribal.

BEN: What are you, some kind of anthropologist?

MARIA: Yes.

BEN: You're an anthropologist?

MARIA: I'm probably the most famous anthropologist in the world.

BEN: Really? How come I don't recognise you?

MARIA: Do you follow anthropology?

BEN shakes his head.

MARIA: Basically, I'm the Taylor Swift of the anthropology world.

BEN is briefly intrigued.

BEN: You serious?

MARIA nods, then BEN remembers he's in a huff.

BEN: I hate Taylor Swift.

MARIA: Look, I'm sorry I upset you. Sometimes I just forget how clever I am compared to other people.

BEN: Shove it up your arse. That's if you can take your head out of it.

MARIA: Aw, c'mon, you're making me feel bad now. Let's go back to our wee game, eh? I ruined it. I know I did. I'm sorry. Come on, hit me with a question.

BEN: Ever had your heart broken?

A silence blooms between them.

MARIA: Oh. You're not fucking about now, are you?

BEN: Nope.

MARIA: Well well well.

A respect is growing in her eyes.

MARIA: I suppose there's no point getting to know folk superficially. Alright then, buddy boy. Let's go deeper.

BEN: Culture of honesty.

MARIA: Culture of honesty. Exactly. Yes, I've had my heart broken. Of course I have.

BEN: By who?

MARIA: Know how you asked me about finding myself in a room with a button marked Do Not Press?

BEN: Yes.

MARIA: Well. I found myself in a room just like that. A lovely, big hotel room just like that.

BEN: And you pressed it?

MARIA: *(Shows the crucifix.)* Let's just say that's why I wear this now. To ward off vampires.

BEN: I see. Sorry, I didn't mean to bring back bad memor–

MARIA: Have *you* ever had your heart broken?

BEN pauses, then nods.

MARIA: What age were you?

BEN: Twenty-one.

MARIA: Oh. Oh right. This is *that* story. What was her name?

BEN: His name.

MARIA: His name?

BEN: Yeah.

MARIA: Wait a minute. Are you *gay?*

BEN: Was that not obvious?

MARIA: How could it be obvious? I thought you were cracking onto me!

BEN: What, like chatting you up?

MARIA: Yes!

BEN: No no no no no. I'm gay.

MARIA: I know that *now*. That's why I was giving you such a hard time!

BEN: Cos you thought I was straight?

MARIA: Aye, a straight white male. The worst cunt in the world.

BEN: Alright, we'll not get back into that.

MARIA: Mate! Gay! Good for you! Fucking YAAAAS!

BEN: Hang on. Are you a lesbian?

MARIA: I'm a *raging* lesbian! Yaaaaas! WE ARE THE PEOPLE!

BEN: Hahaha. So now we know each other.

MARIA: *Now* we know each other.

BEN: I told you it was worth talking to strangers.

MARIA: Aye, but that's easy for you to say. You're no a woman on public transport. See the amount of pish we have to put up with? Guys just presuming they have a right to chat to you, that you owe it to them. 'C'mon, hen, give us a wee smile!' So I just use them as sport. Rip them to bits, just to teach them a lesson.

BEN: That's what you were doing to me?

MARIA: Aye, but I would never have done it to my own kind, pal. Just to these straight wankers. So, c'mon, tell me. What happened?

BEN: What happened when?

MARIA: Who broke your heart? What did he do?

BEN: Oh that. Well, em. He was a straight guy actually.

MARIA: I told you! They're the worst!

BEN: It's like you said, when you're in that room…don't press that button.

MARIA: No, I never said don't press it. You should still press it. Don't let *those* bastards win. Look what happened when you pressed this button. I spoke to you. Now we're pals.

BEN: Ach, I think I just got scared after that. I've always found it hard to talk to other men, even gay ones. Too many…consequences.

MARIA: 'Too many consequences'. You need to toughen up, mate. You take what *you* need from a lover then tell them to fuck off.

BEN: That's not me.

MARIA: Let me tell you something, there's the shaggers and the shagged. And you, my friend, are the shagged.

BEN: I suppose you're a shagger?

MARIA: My mum ran around after my dad all her life. She died of a heart attack while he was in bed with a twenty-four-year-old. To hell with that.

BEN: Alright, if you're so tough, how did you manage to have your heart broken?

MARIA: Once. ONCE. I'm no gonnay be swooning like a wee schoolgirl after some woman who doesn't care the first thing about me. Never again. Not after that kind of pain. What I learned is that it's better to be the lioness, picking up the lion cub in its mouth, than to be the one getting carried about, and then dropped.

BEN: I hadn't thought of it like that. Maybe you're right. Maybe all my life I've been…been…

MARIA: Getting shagged?

BEN: Getting shagged.

MARIA: That's the problem. If the shaggers only shagged the shaggers and the shagged only shagged the shagged then nobody would get hurt.

BEN: Everyone understands the rules?

MARIA: Exactly.

TERRY comes back from the toilet and sits at the table where his beer is, then starts drinking. He puts his earphones in and starts listening to dance music, its faint, tribal beat underscoring the action. BEN notices. MARIA notices him noticing.

MARIA: Oh. Oh. How interesting.

BEN: What?

MARIA: You fancy him.

BEN: What makes you say that?

MARIA: Cos I'm the fucking Taylor Swift of the anthropology world. Am I right though?

BEN: Let's just if say I was a cat I would purr.

They both laugh.

MARIA: You are a cat. You're a big cat. You're a lion.

BEN: What are you saying?

MARIA: Now's your chance.

BEN: For what?

MARIA: On you go. Press the button.

BEN: You want me to go and talk to him?

MARIA: No, *you* want you to go and talk to him.

BEN: I can't do that.

MARIA: And those are the words…of the shagged.

BEN: It's not that. I can't just…go up to somebody.

MARIA: You talked to me, didn't you? Out of the blue. What's the difference?

BEN: You're a woman. It's easier to talk to women.

MARIA: Oh, like I made it easy for you.

BEN: What if he doesn't want to talk to me?

MARIA: In an empty carriage, why did he sit at that table? The one right next to you?

BEN: And you. He might be straight.

MARIA: So *all the more reason.* Remember that guy who broke your heart? The straight one?

BEN: Yeah.

MARIA: Doesn't at least part of you…want to get your own back?

BEN is thinking about it.

BEN: He did wink at me. *And* he slapped my arm.

MARIA: Take what you want, then throw him away.

BEN: Be the lion?

MARIA: BE THE LION. Put him in your mouth.

She winks. BEN likes this idea.

BEN: Fuck it.

MARIA: Yaaas! Go on, my son!

BEN waves over at TERRY. TERRY looks up.

BEN: Hi.

TERRY takes his earphones out. The dance music cuts out.

TERRY: Eh, hi?

MARIA is giving BEN the thumbs up. He goes for it.

BEN: Me and my friend there–

MARIA smiles sweetly at TERRY.

BEN: – were just having a discussion, and I eh, wanted to get your opinion on something.

TERRY: My opinion about what?

BEN: What's your favourite race?

MARIA facepalms.

TERRY: My favourite what?

BEN: Your favourite race. Y'know, black, white, brown…

TERRY: And how is that your business?

BEN: Oh, are you afraid to answer?

TERRY: Eh, I don't know you. I don't have to answer a thing.

BEN: Well, no, you don't. But that's very telling, isn't it?

TERRY: Excuse me?

MARIA is cutting her hand across her throat trying to get BEN to quit. He doesn't notice.

BEN: I mean, it's just a simple question. It's not like people don't have a favourite race. Why don't you just admit it?

TERRY: Mate, I'm not in the mood.

BEN: Looks like somebody's got something to hide…

TERRY: *(To MARIA.)* Is he for real?

MARIA holds up her hands.

BEN: Alright, alright, I'll give you another one…what do you think of *Brothers in Arms* by Dire Straits?

TERRY stares at BEN and leans towards him.

TERRY: It's pish.

MARIA: Hey. No it's not.

TERRY looks at MARIA. She's shaking her head.

MARIA: *Brothers in Arms* is not pish.

He looks back at BEN and grins.

TERRY: Hang on, hang on. Is there, like, a hidden camera round here or something? Are youse actors?

MARIA: Everybody's acting. All the time.

TERRY is baffled.

BEN: Okay, let me explain. She and I see each other on this train loads, but we've never spoken. So I introduced myself, we got chatting, and I… I think we've reached a level of mutual understanding. Is that fair to say?

MARIA nods, trying to gauge TERRY's reaction to all this.

TERRY: Right. And?

BEN: And you're the only other person on this carriage, so I thought why not include you? Just being neighbourly.

TERRY: Do you go round asking all your neighbours what their favourite race is? Cos if you did that where I live you'd have your baws wrapped round a lamppost.

BEN: Okay the race thing…that was a clumsy opening.

TERRY: Oh, you think?

BEN: I'm sorry about that.

TERRY: But to answer your question, it's white people.

MARIA: Is it?

TERRY: Aye. They're my favourite.

Awkward beat. BEN tries to change the subject.

BEN: Anyway, Dire Straits. We discovered *Brothers in Arms* is an album we both love. So that's why I was asking what you think of it.

TERRY: I don't like it.

BEN: Okay why not?

TERRY: It's just for boring cunts.

MARIA: Boring cunts? Like us?

TERRY: Naw, naw, I don't mean youse. I just mean…folk *like* youse.

MARIA: What do you mean, folk like us?

TERRY: Well youse are both wearing…business gear, eh?

MARIA: What's wrong with that?

TERRY: Nae offence, like, but business folks are just, like, too…straight.

BEN: Too 'straight'?

MARIA and BEN share a knowing laugh.

TERRY: Ken, like just aw…right angles?

He's not sure he's explaining himself properly.

TERRY: I'll gie yese an example. I had this mate, right. Daniel. And we were tight, like. Used to be in the casuals, when we were young and daft. And see when he was in the casuals, his taste in music was sound as fuck. Like, The Specials. Oasis. Bit of techno when we were out on the eckies. Then he got this new burd, Sarah, and she tried tay like straighten him oot, eh? Stopped him seeing aw his mates. He took a joab at an insurance firm, they bought a hoose the gither. So we'd no seen him for ages an I goes roond, and it's oan this like, fancy estate an aw that. And he opens the door and he's like… 'Terry, mate, how's it going?' And fae behind him in the hoose I can hear fuckin… Dire Straits. And I'm like 'Aw, Daniel. Daniel. Whit have you become?'

MARIA: You don't think it was a healthy lifestyle choice for him to quit the casuals?

TERRY: It wasnay so much that. I mean, he was shit in a fight anyway. It's just that he started…looking doon on us. Like we were just… thugs.

BEN: But you *were* thugs. That's the definition of being a football casual.

TERRY: Aye, I know. But we werenay *just* thugs. That's my point. We were also his mates. But I suppose I should have seen it comin eh? I mean, his name wis *Daniel*. Eftir that, the crew kinday broke up. Folk went their separate ways. Stevie ended up dealin the ching, Tam got a joab in the bookies, I joined the army.

BEN: Oh really? My dad was in the army.

TERRY: Whit division?

BEN: Scots Guards.

TERRY: 52nd Lowland. Sixth battalion. Respect tae yer auld man.

He shakes BEN's hand.

BEN: Respect to you. Terry?

TERRY: Aye.

BEN: I'm Ben.

TERRY: Nice to meet you, Ben.

BEN: This is…

He realises something.

BEN: Actually, I don't think I've even asked your name!

MARIA: Typical man.

They all laugh.

MARIA: It's Maria.

BEN: Maria.

They shake hands.

TERRY: Here, yese wantin a beer?

BEN: Oh. Why not eh?

MARIA shrugs.

TERRY: Yaas!

He cracks open the other two beers and hands them one each, then raises his bottle.

MARIA: Em, what are we toasting?

TERRY: New pals. May their burds never straighten them.

MARIA: I'll drink to that.

They clink and swig.

BEN: You see? You see what happens when we press the button and talk to other strangers. What a positive thing. We all know each other's names, you know my Dad was in the army, we know about what happened with you and your mate. We even know why you don't like *Brothers in Arms* by Dire Straits, haha.

TERRY: Aye, basically it's for poofs.

BEN: What's that?

TERRY: That's what happened to Daniel. His burd turned him into a poof.

MARIA: How does that work?

TERRY: You tell me! But I blame that fuckin album haha.

MARIA: Does *Brothers in Arms* by Dire Straits make people gay? Oh hang on, there might be something in that...

She refers to herself and BEN.

TERRY: Are youse poofs, like?

MARIA: No, there's neither of us 'poofs'. He's a gay man and I'm a lesbian.

TERRY: Aw. Right. Well, eh, behind closed doors and aw that eh?

MARIA: But we're not behind closed doors. We're in public.

BEN: So you obviously didn't sit down at that table because I was sitting here?

TERRY: Eh naw, why would I do that?

BEN: The carriage is empty, but you sat down next to us.

TERRY: You want me to be honest?

BEN: Well, we are going for a...culture of honesty.

TERRY: I liked the look of her.

MARIA: 'Her?'

BEN: Do you not think that's a wee bit creepy?

TERRY: Well why did you sit down next to her?

BEN: Cos I wanted to try and talk to her.

MARIA: 'Her?'

TERRY: That's the same reason I sat near her.

MARIA: *'Her?'*

BEN: Aye, but I'm gay.

TERRY: *(To MARIA.)* Did you know he was gay when he started talking to you?

MARIA: Actually, no.

TERRY: So it's just as fuckin creepy then eh? Only when a straight guy does it, it's like – ho! Call the cops, there's a predator on the loose for sittin near a lassie oan a train.

MARIA: Women don't get hassle off gay guys. Just guys like you.

TERRY: Guys like me? But *he's* the one who started talking to you, while I sat here minding my own business.

He's got them there.

TERRY: In fact, *youse* are the ones that started hassling *me*, coming over and hammering me with questions, then getting pissed off when I tell you the answers? Fuck off out ma face, ya poofs.

MARIA: I told you, we're not 'poofs'.

TERRY: Sorry, fuck off out ma face, ya DYKE.

BEN: What you got against gay people? Who are we harming?

TERRY: It's unnatural.

MARIA: *(To BEN.)* See? Straight, white men. Absolute cunts.

TERRY: You just call me a cunt?

MARIA: No, cunts are useful.

TERRY: What did you say?

He stands up. BEN steps between them.

BEN: Sit back down.

TERRY: You better warn your bitch to shut up.

MARIA: I'm nobody's fucking bitch, mate.

TERRY: *(To BEN.)* That why you started talking to me, eh? You trying to get me to be aw…gay?

BEN: Don't be ridiculous.

MARIA: Well, no, technically he's right.

TERRY: Ih?

MARIA: He *was* trying to get you to be gay. Just for a night. But I don't think you could handle it.

TERRY: So do I look like some kind of bum boy to you, mate?

BEN: Well you must do. Cos I wouldn't have chatted you up otherwise.

MARIA: Gon *yersel*, Ben!

TERRY: You'd better get the fuck away from me or I swear to god I'll–

BEN: You'll what? There's a CCTV camera there and there. You lay a finger on either of us it'll not take long to convict you of homophobic assault. Know what's in that briefcase? I'm a lawyer. She's an anthropologist. Who they gonnay believe? This reaches a court, you don't stand a chance.

TERRY: This is unreal. I'm just minding my own business and you rock up to ME, try and crack onto ME, then when I don't play ball you start making threats? Calling me a cunt? And now you're throwing aw this fuckin weight about?

MARIA: Congratulations. Now you know what it feels like to be a woman *every single day*.

BEN: Know what, pal? You remind me of somebody.

TERRY: Aye? Who?

BEN: Guy I used to know. Had all your swagger. He turned out to be a prick as well. Now for the last time… SIT THE FUCK DOWN!

BEN pulls himself up to his full height. TERRY holds up his hands to quell BEN's rage.

TERRY: Alright, big fella, calm down, calm down, we're just talking, awright?

BEN stands there, breathing hard, starting at TERRY. Gradually he starts to calm down.

MARIA advances slowly and puts her face to BEN's.

MARIA: Who's the poof now, eh?

TERRY smacks MARIA right in the face. She staggers backwards. BEN is on him. He grabs TERRY and hauls him down onto the ground, where he starts laying into him. MARIA joins in, kicking him.

BEN: Aye, where's your big homophobic mouth now, ya arsehole!

MARIA: That's from Dire fucking Straits!

The two of them blooter and punch TERRY until he lies motionless.

They stand there, breathing and looking down at TERRY, before BEN takes stock of the situation.

BEN: Holy shit.

MARIA: It's fine. He punched me first. You were just defending me.

BEN: Fucking hell. Fucking hell…

MARIA: How did it feel though, eh? Being the lion?

BEN: Felt good.

MARIA: Did you feel that? You just knocked out a squaddie.

BEN: I did. Yeah.

TRAIN ANNOUNCER *(OFF STAGE.)* We have now arrived at Glasgow Queen Street.

MARIA: You'd better get your stuff ready. Let's not hang about.

BEN: Oh right, shit yeah, of course.

He starts grabbing his stuff, while TERRY moans on the floor. Normality is starting to bleed back in.

BEN: Right. Listen. We need to report this to the police.

MARIA: Why?

BEN: If we leave the scene it'll look suspicious. We'll give our statements, and the cameras will back up that he hit you first. We'll be covered if it reaches court. Trust me, I know what I'm talking about.

MARIA: Ben?

She points at him.

MARIA: You *are* a shagger.

He nods, then exits.

TERRY moans and MARIA kneels to him.

MARIA: You just need to be more careful in future, alright? You can't just say whatever you like. Okay?

TERRY gives another moan that sounds like assent.

MARIA: Good.

She stands, gets her bag and looks down at him, touching her jaw where he punched her.

MARIA: We always have to be learning.

She walks off the train leaving TERRY lying there.

The End.